spicy

spicy

LESLEY MACKLEY

a delicious collection of
classic and contemporary
recipes using spices from
around the world

southwater

This edition is published by Southwater

Distributed in the UK by
The Manning Partnership
251–253 London Road East
Batheaston
Bath BA1 7RL
tel. 01225 852 727
fax 01225 852 852

Published in the USA by
Anness Publishing Inc.
27 West 20th Street
Suite 504 New York NY 10011
fax 212 807 6813

Distributed in Canada by
General Publishing
895 Don Mills Road
400–402 Park Centre
Toronto, Ontario M3C 1W3
tel. 416 445 3333
fax 416 445 5991

Distributed in Australia by
Sandstone Publishing
Unit 1, 360 Norton Street
Leichhardt
New South Wales 2040
tel. 02 9560 7888
fax 02 9560 7488

Southwater is an imprint of Anness Publishing Limited
Hermes House, 88–89 Blackfriars Road, London SE1 8HA
tel. 020 7401 2077; fax 020 7633 9499

© Anness Publishing Limited 2001

Publisher: Joanna Lorenz
Managing Editor: Judith Simons
Senior Editor: Doreen Palamartschuk
Indexer: Hilary Bird
Designer: Annie Moss
Jacket Design: The Bridgewater Book Company Limited
Photographer: William Adams-Lingwood assisted by Louise Dare
Home Economist: Lucy McKelvie assisted by Alison Austin
Praduction Controller: Yolande Denny

Previously published as part of a larger volume *The Spice Ingredients Cookbook*

1 3 5 7 9 10 8 6 4 2

NOTES

Bracketed terms are intended for American readers.

For all recipes, quantities are given in both metric and imperial measures and, where appropriate, measures are also given in
standard cups and spoons. Follow one set, but not a mixture, because they are not interchangeable.

Standard spoon and cup measures are level.
1 tsp = 5ml, 1 tbsp = 15ml, 1 cup = 250ml/8fl oz

Australian standard tablespoons are 20ml. Australian readers should use
3 tsp in place of 1 tbsp for measuring small quantities of gelatine, flour, salt, etc.

Medium (US large) eggs are used unless otherwise stated.

Contents

Cooking with Spices

Choosing and Preparing Spices

What is a spice? Spices are the dried seeds (cumin, coriander, cardamom, mustard), buds (cloves), fruit or flower parts (peppercorns, allspice), bark and roots (cassia, cinnamon and ginger) or leaves (kaffir lime leaves, curry leaves) of plants. They are usually of tropical origin, and almost all are native to Asia. There are exceptions: allspice, vanilla and chillies were originally found in tropical Central America and the Caribbean.

CHOOSING SPICES

When buying spices, select whole seeds, berries, buds and bark, such as cumin seeds, cardamoms, peppercorns, all-spice, cloves, cassia and cinnamon sticks, if you can, as these keep their flavour and pungency far longer than the powdered spices, and can be ground easily as needed. Fresh roots, such as ginger and galangal, and fresh lemon grass are essential for some dishes and have an entirely different flavour to the dried versions.

PREPARATION TECHNIQUES

Spices are prepared in many ways, depending on the form of the spice and the dish in which it's being used – the intention, however is always the same: to release the optimum amount of flavour and aroma.

Dry-frying

This process, sometimes called dry roasting, and often used in Indian cooking, increases the flavour of such spices as cumin, coriander, fennel, mustard and poppy seeds.

Heat a small heavy pan over a medium heat for about 1 minute, then put in the whole spices and cook for 2–3 minutes, stirring or shaking the pan frequently to prevent the spices from burning, or until the spices start to give off a warm, rich aroma.

Remove the pan from the heat and tip the spices into a bowl and grind finely in a mortar with a pestle.

Frying in Oil

Whole spices are sometimes fried in oil, either at the beginning of a recipe, before other ingredients are added, or simply to flavour the oil.

Grinding

Spices are frequently crushed or ground to release their flavour and aroma. Only a few, notably mace, dried ginger and turmeric, cinnamon and cassia, are hard to grind at home and usually bought in powdered form. For the best flavour, grind spices as you need them. Do not grind them more than a day or two in advance.

For small, easily ground dried spices, such as cumin, fennel, caraway seeds and cloves, use an earthenware mortar and pestle. Grind only a small amount at a time – do not put more than a table-spoon or two in the bowl at a time, and grind in a circular motion.

Coriander seeds and allspice, and some harder spices, such as fenugreek, can be ground successfully in a pepper mill. Special nutmeg grinders, similar to pepper mills are also available and work fairly well.

An easier and quicker method of grinding these harder spices is to use an electric coffee grinder. Do not over-fill the bowl, and grind in short bursts.

Fresh ingredients, such as ginger and garlic, and larger spices, such as chillies, can be easily ground using a mortar and pestle. Traditional Indian and Asian mortars have pitted or ridged bowls and are good for making wet spice mixtures and pastes.

Wet spice mixtures can also be made in a food processor. Use the metal blade, add the ingredients and process to a rough or smooth paste as required. Slicing the ingredients into small pieces before adding to the processor will result in a smoother paste. If the ingredients are all dry, add a little of the oil from the recipe to help the processing.

PREPARING CHILLIES

Chillies need to be handled carefully. If you have sensitive skin, or are preparing a lot of chillies, it is worth wearing rubber gloves. Do not touch your eyes or mouth while you work, and always wash your hands and cooking implements after preparing chillies. It is easier to seed chillies before chopping: cut the chilli in half and scrape out the seeds using the point of a knife.

Grating

Fresh root spices, such as horseradish and ginger, and whole nutmegs are grated before use.

To grate ginger or horseradish, peel the root, then grate it on the fine blade of a stainless steel grater.

Grate nutmegs on a special nutmeg grater or on the finest blade of a standard grater.

Bruising and Crushing

Some spices, such as cardamom, juniper, ginger and lemon grass, are often lightly crushed to release their aroma or, in the case of cardamom, to release the seeds for crushing. Garlic is often crushed rather than chopped.

Juniper berries and cardamoms are easily crushed using a mortar and pestle. (Alternatively, place them in a sturdy plastic bag and crush them with a rolling pin.)

Fresh ginger, galangal or lemon grass, which are to be added whole to a recipe during cooking for a subtle flavour and then removed before serving, can be bruised with one or two sharp blows, until the fibres are crushed, on a chopping board using the flat blade of a large knife, or a large pestle.

A simple and effective way of crushing garlic cloves is to trim off the root end and place the unpeeled clove cut-end down in a garlic press. After the garlic is crushed, the skin can simply be removed, making cleaning the press very easy.

Shredding and Chopping

Some fresh spices, such as ginger, garlic and kaffir lime leaves, are cut into thin slices or pieces before use to maximize the flavour and aroma.

Kaffir lime leaves are usually shredded rather than chopped. Hold one or two leaves together on a chopping board and cut into fine strips using a small sharp knife.

To chop ginger, cut the peeled root lengthwise into thin slices, then slice again into long strips. Hold a few strips together at a time and chop finely.

Infusing

One or two spices are always infused (steeped) in a warm liquid before use. When saffron is infused it imparts not only a wonderful aroma, but also a vibrant yellow colour. Tamarind is infused to produce a tangy juice that is used in a similar way to lemon juice or vinegar to add sharpness to a dish.

To infuse saffron threads, warm a little milk, water or liquid from the recipe. Add the saffron and leave to infuse for about 5 minutes. Do not strain the liquid; both threads and liquid are used in the recipe.

To infuse tamarind pulp, place a small piece of the pulp in a jug (pitcher) or bowl, add 60ml/4 tbsp warm water and leave for 10 minutes.

Mix with the fingers to loosen the purée from the seeds, then strain through a nylon sieve. Discard the pulp and seeds and use the juice as directed in the recipe.

PREPARING SHRIMP PASTE

Blachan, also called trassi or terasi, is not a spice, but a strong smelling, firm paste made of fermented shrimps that is used in South-east Asian cooking. It can be bought in Asian stores. Unless it is to be fried as part of a recipe, shrimp paste is always lightly cooked before use. If you have a gas stove, simply mould the paste on to the end of a metal skewer and rotate over a low to medium gas flame, or heat the piece of paste under the grill (broiler) of an electric stove, until the outside begins to look crusty but not burnt. To avoid the strong smell filling the kitchen, wrap the paste in foil and fry in a dry frying pan over a gentle heat for 4–5 minutes, turning from time to time.

Equipment for Preparing Spices

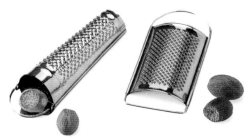

Spices are often ground, crushed, pounded or puréed to create powders and pastes. Although these processes are simple, there are a few useful items of equipment that make these tasks much easier.

Nutmeg graters come in a variety of shapes and sizes. They have very fine rough holes and produce a fine powder. The one on the left doubles as a storage container.

Smooth earthenware mortars and pestles come in a variety of sizes and are excellent for grinding small amounts of dry spices.

Traditional Indian and Asian granite or stone pestles and mortars are generally fairly large, with deep, pitted or ridged bowls. They are ideal for pounding fresh spices, such as ginger, galangal and lemon grass, as the rough surface seems to grip the pieces and prevents them flying out of the bowl as you pound the mixture.

Bigger, flat-bowled mortars and pestles are particularly good for making spice pastes that include large amounts of fresh spices, herbs, onion and garlic.

A simple garlic press makes quick work of crushing garlic cloves.

An electric coffee grinder is excellent for grinding dry spices. If you are going to do a lot of spice cooking, it is worth keeping a separate grinder purely for this purpose.

Electric food processors come into their own for making larger quantities of spice pastes and purées.

Nutmeg mills work by rotating the nutmeg over a blade – different models grate with varying degrees of success.

This small clear Perspex (Plexiglas) mill can be used to grind both cinnamon and cassia bark.

Traditional Japanese ginger graters make light work of grating ginger and are easy to clean. A stainless steel box grater works equally well – use the finest grating surface and work over a flat plate to catch the juices.

How to Store Spices

Very few cooks store spices correctly. Dried spices are usually displayed in glass jars on the kitchen shelf or in wall racks, and fresh spices, such as ginger or lemon grass, are often kept on a kitchen shelf or in a vegetable rack, sometimes in a sunny spot or under bright lights. Here are some tips on how to preserve the flavour and aroma of your spices.

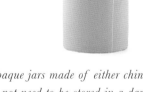

STORING FRESH SPICES

Unless you are going to use fresh spices the day they are bought, they should be chilled rather than stored at room temperature. Lemon grass, kaffir lime leaves and curry leaves are best wrapped in a piece of kitchen paper and stored in the salad drawer of the refrigerator for up to 2 weeks. Fresh galangal, ginger and chillies will keep for up to 3 weeks in a sealed container, lined with kitchen paper, in the refrigerator. If you want to keep them longer, fresh spices can be pounded to a paste, then put in sealed containers and frozen for up to 6 months.

STORING DRIED SPICES

Both ground and whole dried spices should be stored in airtight containers in a cool, dark cabinet or drawer as light, heat and moisture lessen their quality. Whole spices will keep for 6 months or even longer, if stored carefully. However, most ground spices lose their colour, flavour and aroma within 5 or 6 months. If you are unsure just how long the spices have been stored, check the aroma – if the spice smells musty, or if there is little aroma, it is likely that the flavour will be impaired, too. It is a good idea to label new jars of spices with the date you bought them.

Opaque jars made of either china or metal do not need to be stored in a dark place, but they are still better kept in a cool cabinet out of the heat of the kitchen.

STORING OTHER SPICES

Bottles or tubes of spice pastes and purées, such as ginger and garlic purée, will keep unopened until the best-before date. However, once opened, they should be stored in the refrigerator and used within 6 weeks. Both dried and ready-made mustard will keep for up to a year, even when opened. Dried tamarind and vanilla pods (beans) will keep in a cool dark place for up to 2 years.

This stainless steel spice container is ideal for storing dried spices. The individual pots are sealed when the inner lid is closed: a second lid ensures that no light or moisture gets into the large container.

Small glass jars with airtight seals or screw tops are perfectly good containers for storing dried spices, providing they are kept in a cool, dark place and not in a rack on the wall or on a kitchen shelf.

Spice Mixtures

Cajun spice mix

Cajun Spice Mix

The name Cajun evolved from the corruption of "Acadian", the French settlers who left Canada after the English took over in 1755. They eventually settled in Louisiana, where the exchange of cooking techniques and dishes between the Creoles and the French began. This spice mixture can be used as a seasoning for the famous jambalaya and gumbo, as well as for fish steaks, chicken or meat. If you plan to make up the mixture in advance, prepare the dry spice ingredients and store them in an airtight container. When the mixture is required, chop the onion and garlic in a food processor and add to the spice mixture.

MAKES ABOUT 150ML/¼ PINT/⅔ CUP
5ml/1 tsp black peppercorns
5ml/1 tsp cumin seeds
5ml/1 tsp white mustard seeds
10ml/2 tsp paprika
5ml/1 tsp chilli powder or
  cayenne pepper
5ml/1 tsp dried oregano
10ml/2 tsp dried thyme
5ml/1 tsp salt
2 garlic cloves
1 onion, sliced

1 Dry-fry or roast the peppercorns, cumin and mustard seeds over a medium heat to release their flavours.

2 Grind the roasted spices to a fine powder, then add the paprika, chilli or cayenne, oregano, thyme and salt and grind again.

3 If the spice mix is to be used immediately, add the spices to the finely chopped garlic and onion in a blender or food processor and process until well combined.

Tadka

Achieving the right balance of ingredients for a curry powder is highly personal. The basic recipe with variations can be adapted to suit your taste and the main ingredients for any particular dish.

MAKES ENOUGH FOR 1 DISH
30ml/2 tbsp ghee
10ml/2 tsp black mustard seeds
2.5ml/½ tsp ground asafoetida
about 8 fresh or dried
  curry leaves

1 Assemble all the ingredients – more curry leaves can be added if you like.

2 Melt the ghee in a frying pan or large pan and have a lid ready to cover the pan. When the ghee is hot add the mustard seeds, which will jump when they pop so be ready to cover the pan with a lid.

3 Draw the pan off the heat and add the asafoetida and curry leaves. Stir and then add to a dhal, soup or stew.

Tadka

Garlic and Spice Aromatic Oil

Bottles for keeping oil must be pristine clean, and cork stoppers are preferable. Wash the bottles well and clean them with a proprietary sterilizing solution if necessary (look for wine-making sterilizing agents or solutions for cleaning babies' bottles), leave upside down on the draining rack to dry completely.

There are no hard and fast rules on the type of oil or the spices to use, except that they should be complementary. For instance, extra virgin olive oil is an ideal oil for Mediterranean spices and herbs; groundnut (peanut) oil goes well with the Eastern

flavours of lemon grass and ginger; nut oils, such as walnut and hazelnut, are wonderful flavoured with coriander seeds and cinnamon sticks for adding to salad dressings to serve with pasta. Remember to label the bottles.

Almost fill a clean bottle with best virgin olive oil. For 600ml/1 pint/ 2½ cups oil, peel and halve a large garlic clove, then add it to the bottle with 3 whole red chillies, 5ml/1 tsp coriander seeds, 3 allspice berries, 6 black peppercorns, 4 juniper berries and 2 bay leaves.

Cover tightly and leave in a cool, dark place for 2 weeks. If the flavour is not sufficiently pronounced, leave the oil for another week before using. Label clearly and store or wrap decoratively as a gift.

Sambal Kecap

This Indonesian sauce or sambal can be served as a dip for satays instead of the usual peanut sauce, particularly with beef and chicken, and it is also good with deep-fried chicken.

<u>MAKES 150ML/¼ PINT/⅔ CUP</u>
1 fresh red chilli, seeded and
** finely chopped**
2 garlic cloves, crushed
60ml/4 tbsp dark soy sauce
20ml/4 tsp lemon juice or
** 15–25ml/1–1½ tbsp**
** tamarind juice**
30ml/2 tbsp hot water
30ml/2 tbsp deep-fried onion
** slices (optional)**

1 Mix the chilli, garlic, soy sauce, lemon or tamarind juice and hot water in a bowl.

2 Stir in the onion slices, if using, and leave to stand for 30 minutes before serving.

Sambal kecap

Seven-seas curry powder

Seven-seas Curry Powder

This relatively mild blend of spices is much enjoyed in Indonesian and Malaysian cooking, for curries, sambals, casseroles and kebabs. The name is derived from the fact that seven seas, including the Andaman and South China Sea, converge on the shores of Malaysia and the thousands of islands that make up the archipelago of Indonesia.

<u>MAKES 200ML/7 FL OZ/SCANT 1 CUP</u>
6–8 white cardamoms
90ml/6 tbsp coriander seeds
45ml/3 tbsp cumin seeds
25ml/1½ tbsp celery seeds
5 cm/2 in piece cinnamon stick
** or cassia**
6–8 cloves
15ml/1 tbsp chilli powder

1 Bruise the cardamom pods and place them in a heavy frying pan with all the other spices except the chilli powder. Dry-fry the mixture, stirring it and shaking the pan continuously, until the spices give off a rich, heady aroma.

2 Remove cardamom seeds from their pods, then grind them with all the other roasted ingredients to a fine powder. Add the chilli powder and mix well.

Tsire Powder

This simple spice mixture is used as a coating for kebabs throughout West Africa. The raw meat is dipped first in oil or beaten egg and then in the spice mixture. Sprinkle a little of the mixture over the cooked meat before serving.

<u>MAKES 60ML/4 TBSP</u>
50g/2oz/½ cup salted peanuts
5ml/1 tsp mixed (pumpkin pie)
** spice**
2.5–5ml/½–1 tsp chilli powder
salt

1 Grind the peanuts to a coarse powder in a mortar, blender or food processor, then add the ground mixed spice, chilli powder and a little salt.

2 Use at once or transfer to an airtight container and store in a cool place for up to 6 weeks.

Tsire powder

<u>COOK'S TIP</u>
Mixed spice is a ready ground, commercial spice mixture, sometimes called pudding spice, that contains allspice, cinnamon, cloves, ginger and nutmeg.

SOUPS AND APPETIZERS

Hot and Sour Prawn Soup

How hot this soup is depends upon the type of chilli used. Try tiny Thai chillies if you really want to go for the burn.

SERVES 6

225g/8oz raw prawns (shrimp)
   in shells
2 lemon grass stalks
1.5 litres/2¹⁄₂ pints/6¹⁄₄ cups
   vegetable stock
4 kaffir lime leaves
2 slices fresh root ginger, peeled
60ml/4 tbsp Thai fish sauce
60ml/4 tbsp fresh lime juice
2 garlic cloves, crushed
6 spring onions
   (scallions), chopped
1 fresh red chilli, seeded and cut
   into thin strips
115g/4oz/generous 1¹⁄₂ cups
   oyster mushrooms, sliced
fresh coriander (cilantro)
   sprigs and kaffir lime slices,
   to garnish

1 Peel the prawns and set them aside. Put the shells in a large pan.

COOK'S TIP

The prawns should be only heated through and not overcooked, or they will become tough.

2 Lightly crush the lemon grass and add the stalks to the pan with the stock, lime leaves and ginger. Bring to the boil, lower the heat and simmer for 20 minutes.

3 Strain the stock into a clean pan, discarding the prawn shells and aromatics. Add the fish sauce, lime juice, garlic, spring onions, chilli and mushrooms. Bring to the boil, lower the heat and simmer for 5 minutes. Add the peeled prawns and cook for 2 minutes to heat through. Garnish with the coriander and lime, and serve.

Provençal Fish Soup with Rouille

Although many of the tiny rock fish traditionally used in this recipe are not available away from the Mediterranean, this version is still full of Provençal flavours and is served with an authentic chilli-spiked rouille.

SERVES 4–6

30ml/2 tbsp olive oil
1 leek, sliced
2 celery sticks, chopped
1 onion, chopped
2 garlic cloves, chopped
4 ripe tomatoes, chopped
15ml/1 tbsp tomato purée (paste)
150ml/¼ pint/⅔ cup dry
  white wine
1 bay leaf
5ml/1 tsp saffron threads
1kg/2¼lb mixed fish fillets and
  prepared shellfish
fish trimmings, bones and heads
salt and ground black pepper
croûtons and grated Gruyère
  cheese, to serve
ROUILLE
1 slice of white bread, crusts
  removed
1 red (bell) pepper, cored, seeded
  and quartered
1–2 fresh red chillies, seeded
  and chopped
2 garlic cloves, crushed
olive oil (optional)

1 Make the rouille. Soak the bread in 30–45ml/2–3 tbsp cold water for 10 minutes. Meanwhile, grill (broil) the red pepper quarters, skin-side up, until the skin is charred and blistered. Put into a plastic bag and leave until cool enough to handle. Peel off the skin. Drain the bread and squeeze out the excess moisture.

2 Roughly chop the pepper quarters and place in a food processor or blender with the bread, chillies and garlic. Process to a fairly coarse paste, adding a little olive oil, if necessary. Scrape the rouille into a small bowl and set it aside.

3 Heat the olive oil in a large pan. Add the leek, celery, onion and garlic. Cook gently for 10 minutes until soft. Add the tomatoes, tomato purée, wine, bay leaf, saffron, any shellfish and the fish trimmings. Bring to the boil, lower the heat, cover and simmer gently for 30 minutes.

4 Strain through a colander, pressing out the liquid. Cut the fish fillets into large chunks and add to the strained soup. Cover and simmer for about 5–10 minutes until the fish is cooked.

5 Strain through a colander into a clean pan. Put half the cooked fish into a blender or food processor with about 300ml/½ pint/1¼ cups of the soup. Process for just long enough to blend, while retaining some texture.

6 Stir all the fish back into the remaining soup. Add salt and pepper to taste. Reheat gently. Serve the soup with the rouille, croûtons and cheese.

Butternut Squash Soup with Curried Horseradish Cream

The combination of cream, curry powder and horseradish makes a wonderful topping for this beautiful golden soup.

SERVES 6

1 butternut squash
1 cooking apple
25g/1oz/2 tbsp butter
1 onion, finely chopped
5–10ml/1–2 tsp curry powder
900ml/1½ pints/3¾ cups chicken
 or vegetable stock
5ml/1 tsp chopped fresh sage
150ml/¼ pint/⅔ cup apple juice
salt and ground black pepper
curry powder and lime shreds
 (optional), to garnish
CURRIED HORSERADISH CREAM
60ml/4 tbsp double (heavy) cream
10ml/2 tsp horseradish sauce
2.5ml/½ tsp curry powder

Spiced Lentil Soup

A subtle blend of spices takes this warming soup to new heights. Serve it with crusty bread for a satisfying lunch.

SERVES 6

2 onions, finely chopped
2 garlic cloves, crushed
4 tomatoes, coarsely chopped
2.5ml/½ tsp ground turmeric
5ml/1 tsp ground cumin
6 cardamoms
½ cinnamon stick
225g/8oz/1 cup red lentils
400g/14oz can coconut milk
15ml/1 tbsp fresh lime juice
salt and ground black pepper
cumin seeds, to garnish

1 Peel the squash, remove the seeds and chop the flesh. Peel, core and chop the apple.

2 Heat the butter in a large pan. Add the onion and cook over a low heat, stirring occasionally, for 5 minutes until soft. Stir in the curry powder. Cook to bring out the flavour, stirring constantly, for 2 minutes.

3 Add the stock, squash, apple and sage. Bring to the boil, lower the heat, cover and simmer for 20 minutes until the squash and apple are soft.

1 Put the onions, garlic, tomatoes, turmeric, cumin, cardamoms, cinnamon and lentils into a pan with 900ml/1½ pints/3¾ cups water. Bring to the boil, lower the heat, cover and simmer gently for about 20 minutes or until the lentils are soft.

2 Remove and discard the cardamoms and cinnamon stick, then purée the mixture thoroughly in a blender or food processor. Press the soup through a sieve, then return it to the clean pan.

4 Meanwhile, make the horseradish cream. Whip the cream in a bowl until stiff, then stir in the horseradish sauce and curry powder. Cover and chill until required.

5 Purée the soup in a blender or food processor. Return to the clean pan and add the apple juice, with salt and pepper to taste. Reheat gently, without allowing the soup to boil.

6 Serve the soup in individual bowls, topping each portion with a spoonful of horseradish cream and a dusting of curry powder. Garnish with a few lime shreds, if you like.

3 Reserve a little of the coconut milk for the garnish and add the remainder to the pan with the lime juice. Stir well. Season with salt and pepper. Reheat the soup gently without boiling. Swirl in the reserved coconut milk, garnish with cumin seeds and serve.

COOK'S TIP

If the tomatoes do not have much flavour, stir in a little tomato purée (paste) or use a small can of tomatoes.

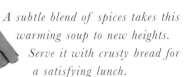

Crab Spring Rolls and Dipping Sauce

Chilli and grated ginger add a hint of heat to these sensational treats. Serve them as an appetizer or with other Chinese dishes.

SERVES 4–6

15ml/1 tbsp groundnut (peanut) oil
5ml/1 tsp sesame oil
1 garlic clove, crushed
1 fresh red chilli, seeded and
 thinly sliced
450g/1lb pack fresh
 stir-fry vegetables
2.5cm/1in piece of fresh root
 ginger, grated
15ml/1 tbsp dry sherry or rice wine
15ml/1 tbsp soy sauce
350g/12oz fresh dressed crab meat
 (brown and white meat)
12 spring roll wrappers
1 small (US medium) egg, beaten
oil, for deep-frying
salt and ground black pepper
lime wedges and fresh coriander
 (cilantro), to garnish
1 quantity Indonesian sambal
 kecap, for dipping

1 Heat a wok briefly, then add the groundnut and sesame oils. When hot, stir-fry the crushed garlic and chilli for 1 minute. Add the vegetables and ginger and stir-fry for 1 minute more, then drizzle over the sherry or rice wine and soy sauce. Allow the mixture to bubble up for 1 minute.

2 Using a slotted spoon, transfer the vegetables to a dish. Set aside until cool, then stir in the crab meat and season with salt and pepper.

COOK'S TIP

Spring roll wrappers are available in many supermarkets as well as Asian grocers. If you are unable to find them, use filo pastry instead. Keep the wrappers – and the filled rolls – covered with clear film (plastic wrap), as they will rapidly dry out if exposed to the air.

3 Soften the spring roll wrappers, following the directions on the packet. Place some of the filling on a wrapper, fold over the front edge and the sides and roll up neatly, sealing the edges with a little beaten egg. Repeat with the remaining wrappers and filling.

4 Heat the oil in the wok and fry the spring rolls in batches, turning several times, until brown and crisp. Remove with a slotted spoon, drain on kitchen paper and keep hot while frying the remainder. Serve at once, garnished with lime wedges and coriander, with the dipping sauce.

Chickpea and Coriander Cakes with Tahini

These spicy little cakes are equally good served hot or cold. For a more substantial snack, tuck them into pockets of pitta bread with salad.

SERVES 4

2 x 425g/15oz cans chickpeas
2 garlic cloves, crushed
1 bunch spring onions (scallions), white parts only, chopped
10ml/2 tsp ground cumin
10ml/2 tsp ground coriander
1 green chilli, seeded and chopped
30ml/2 tbsp chopped fresh coriander (cilantro)
1 small (US medium) egg, beaten
30ml/2 tbsp plain (all-purpose) flour
seasoned flour, for shaping
oil, for shallow frying
salt and ground black pepper
lemon wedges and fresh coriander, to garnish

TAHINI AND LEMON DIP
30ml/2 tbsp tahini
juice of 1 lemon
2 garlic cloves, crushed

1 Drain the chickpeas thoroughly. Tip them into a blender or food processor and process until smooth. Add the garlic, spring onions, cumin and ground coriander. Process again until well mixed.

2 Scrape the mixture into a bowl and stir in the chilli, fresh coriander, egg and flour. Mix well and season with the salt and pepper. If the mixture is very soft add a little more flour. Chill for about 30 minutes to firm the mixture.

3 Make the dip. Mix the tahini, lemon juice and garlic in a bowl, adding a little water if the sauce is too thick. Set aside.

4 Using floured hands, shape the chickpea mixture into 12 cakes. Heat the oil in a frying pan and fry the cakes in batches for about 1 minute on each side, until crisp and golden. Drain on kitchen paper and serve with the dip and lemon and coriander garnish.

VARIATION

Another quick sauce is made by mixing Greek (US strained, plain) yogurt with a little chopped chilli and fresh mint.

Spiced Dolmades

These dolmades contain sumac, a spice with a sharp lemon flavour. It is available from specialist food stores.

MAKES 20

**20 vacuum-packed vine leaves
  in brine
90g/3½oz/½ cup long grain rice
45ml/3 tbsp olive oil
1 small onion, finely chopped
50g/2oz/⅔ cup pine nuts
45ml/3 tbsp raisins
30ml/2 tbsp chopped fresh mint
2.5ml/½ tsp ground cinnamon
2.5ml/½ tsp ground allspice
10ml/2 tsp ground sumac
10ml/2 tsp lemon juice
30ml/2 tbsp tomato purée (paste)
salt and ground black pepper
lemon slices and fresh mint
  sprigs, to garnish**

1 Rinse the vine leaves well under cold running water, then drain. Bring a pan of lightly salted water to the boil. Add the rice, lower the heat, cover and simmer for 10–12 minutes, until almost cooked. Drain.

2 Heat 2 tbsp of the olive oil in a frying pan, add the onion and cook until soft. Stir in the pine nuts and cook until lightly browned, then add the raisins, mint, cinnamon, allspice and sumac, with salt and pepper to taste. Stir in the rice and mix well. Leave to cool.

VARIATION

Fresh vine leaves may be used, but must be blanched in boiling water first to make them pliable.

3 Line a pan with any damaged vine leaves. Trim the stalks from the remaining vine leaves and lay them flat. Place a little of the filling on each leaf. Fold the sides over and roll up each leaf neatly. Place the dolmades side by side in the leaf-lined pan, so that they fit tightly.

4 Mix 300ml/½ pint/1¼ cups water with the lemon juice and tomato purée in a bowl. Add the remaining olive oil. Pour the mixture over the dolmades and place a heatproof plate on top to keep them in place.

5 Cover the pan and simmer the dolmades for 1 hour until all the liquid has been absorbed and the leaves are tender. Transfer to a platter, garnish with lemon slices and mint and serve hot or cold.

Marinated Feta Cheese with Capers

Marinating cubes of feta cheese with herbs and spices gives a marvellous flavour. Serve on toast or with salad.

SERVES 6

**350g/12oz/2 cups feta cheese
2 garlic cloves
2.5ml/½ tsp mixed peppercorns
8 coriander seeds
1 bay leaf
15–30ml/1–2 tbsp drained capers
fresh oregano or thyme sprigs
olive oil, to cover
hot toast, to serve**

1 Cut the feta cheese into cubes. Thickly slice the garlic. Mix the peppercorns and coriander seeds in a mortar and crush lightly with a pestle.

2 Pack the feta cubes into a large preserving jar with the bay leaf, interspersing layers of cheese with garlic, crushed peppercorns and coriander, capers and the fresh oregano or thyme sprigs.

3 Pour in enough olive oil to cover the cheese. Close tightly and marinate for 2 weeks in the refrigerator.

4 Lift out the feta cubes and serve on hot toast, sprinkled with a little of the oil from the jar.

VARIATION

Add pitted black or green olives to the feta cheese in the marinade.

Spicy Potato Wedges with Chilli Dip

For a healthy snack with superb flavour, try these dry-roasted potato wedges. The crisp spice crust makes them irresistible, especially when served with a chilli dip.

SERVES 2

2 baking potatoes, about
   225g/8oz each
30ml/2 tbsp olive oil
2 garlic cloves, crushed
5ml/1 tsp ground allspice
5ml/1 tsp ground coriander
15ml/1 tbsp paprika
salt and ground black pepper
CHILLI DIP
15ml/1 tbsp olive oil
1 small onion, finely chopped
1 garlic clove, crushed
200g/7oz can chopped tomatoes
1 fresh red chilli, seeded
   and chopped
15ml/1 tbsp balsamic vinegar
15ml/1 tbsp chopped fresh
   coriander (cilantro), plus extra
   to garnish

1 Preheat the oven to 200°C/400°F/ Gas 6. Cut the potatoes in half, then into 8 wedges.

2 Place the wedges in a pan of cold water. Bring to the boil, then lower the heat and simmer gently for 10 minutes or until the potatoes have softened slightly. Drain well and pat dry on kitchen paper.

3 Mix the oil, garlic, allspice, coriander and paprika in a roasting pan. Add salt and pepper to taste. Add the potatoes to the pan and shake to coat them thoroughly. Roast, turning the potato wedges occasionally, for 20 minutes or until they are browned, crisp and fully cooked.

4 Meanwhile, make the chilli dip. Heat the oil in a pan, add the onion and garlic and cook for 5–10 minutes until soft. Add the tomatoes, with their juice. Stir in the chilli and vinegar. Cook gently for 10 minutes until the mixture has reduced and thickened, then check the seasoning. Stir in the fresh coriander and serve hot, with potato wedges. Garnish with salt and fresh coriander.

COOK'S TIP

To save time, par-boil the potatoes and toss them with the spices in advance, but make sure that the potato wedges are perfectly dry and completely covered in the mixture.

Baby Onions and Mushrooms à la Grecque

There are many variations of this classic dish, but they always contain coriander seeds.

SERVES 4

2 carrots
375g/12oz baby (pearl) onions
60ml/4 tbsp olive oil
120ml/4fl oz/½ cup dry
  white wine
5ml/1 tsp coriander seeds,
  lightly crushed
2 bay leaves
pinch of cayenne pepper
1 garlic clove, crushed
375g/13oz button mushrooms
3 tomatoes, peeled, seeded
  and quartered
salt and ground black pepper
45ml/3 tbsp chopped fresh flat-
  leaf parsley, to garnish

1 Peel the carrots and cut them into small dice. Peel the baby onions and trim the tops and roots.

2 Heat 45ml/3 tbsp of the olive oil in a deep frying pan. Add the carrots and onions and cook, stirring occasionally, for about 20 minutes until all the vegetables have browned lightly and are beginning to soften.

3 Add the white wine, coriander seeds, bay leaves, cayenne, garlic, mushrooms and tomatoes, with salt and pepper to taste. Cook, uncovered, for 20–30 minutes until the vegetables are soft and the sauce has thickened.

COOK'S TIP

Don't trim too much from either the top or root end of the onions: if you do, the centres will pop out during cooking.

4 Transfer to a serving dish and leave to cool. Cover and chill until needed. Before serving, pour over the remaining olive oil and sprinkle with the parsley. Serve with crusty bread.

VARIATION

This treatment is ideal for a single vegetable or a combination. Try leeks, fennel or artichokes, with or without baby onions.

FISH AND SHELLFISH

Mussels and Clams with Lemon Grass and Coconut Cream

Lemon grass has a unique flavour and is widely used in Thai cooking. If you have difficulty getting the clams for this recipe, use a few extra mussels instead.

SERVES 6

1.8kg/4lb mussels
450g/1lb baby clams
120ml/4fl oz/¹⁄₂ cup white wine
1 bunch spring onions (scallions), chopped
2 lemon grass stalks, chopped
6 kaffir lime leaves, chopped
10ml/2 tsp Thai green curry paste
200ml/7fl oz/1 cup coconut cream
30ml/2 tbsp chopped fresh coriander (cilantro)
salt and ground black pepper
garlic chives, to garnish

1 Clean the mussels by pulling off the beards, scrubbing the shells well and removing any barnacles. Discard any mussels that are broken or which do not close when tapped sharply. Wash the clams.

2 Put the wine in a large pan with the spring onions, lemon grass, lime leaves and curry paste. Simmer until the wine has almost evaporated.

COOK'S TIP

Buy a few extra mussels in case there are any that have to be discarded.

3 Add the mussels and clams to the pan, cover tightly and steam the shellfish over a high heat for 5–6 minutes, until they open.

4 Using a slotted spoon, transfer the mussels and clams to a heated serving bowl and keep hot. Discard any shellfish that remain closed. Strain the cooking liquid into a clean pan and simmer to reduce to about 250ml/8fl oz/1 cup.

5 Stir in the coconut cream and coriander, with salt and pepper to taste. Heat through. Pour the sauce over the mussels and clams and serve, garnished with garlic chives.

Sardines in Escabeche

This spicy marinade is widely used in Spain and Portugal as a traditional means of preserving fish, poultry or game. It is good with fried fish.

SERVES 2–4

16 sardines, cleaned
seasoned flour
30ml/2 tbsp olive oil
roasted red onion, green (bell)
  pepper and tomatoes, to garnish
MARINADE
90ml/6 tbsp olive oil
1 onion, sliced
1 garlic clove, crushed
3–4 bay leaves
2 cloves
1 dried red chilli
5ml/1 tsp paprika
120ml/4fl oz/½ cup wine or
  sherry vinegar
120ml/4fl oz/½ cup white wine
salt and ground black pepper

1 Cut the heads off the sardines and split each of them along the belly. Turn them over so that the backbone is uppermost. Press down along the backbone to loosen it, then carefully lift out the backbone and as many remaining bones as possible.

2 Close the sardines up again and dust them with seasoned flour. Heat the olive oil in a frying pan and fry the sardines for 2–3 minutes on each side. Remove the fish from the pan and allow to cool, then place in a single layer in a large shallow dish.

VARIATION

White fish can be prepared in this way, but the method is particularly successful with oily fish such as herrings or sprats.

3 To make the marinade, add the olive oil to the oil remaining in the frying pan. Fry the onion and garlic gently for 5–10 minutes until soft. Add the bay leaves, cloves, chilli and paprika, with pepper to taste. Fry, stirring, for another 1–2 minutes.

4 Stir in the vinegar, wine and a little salt. Allow to bubble up, then pour over the sardines. When cool, cover and chill overnight or for up to 3 days. Serve, garnished with roasted onion, pepper and tomatoes.

Cajun Blackened Fish with Papaya Salsa

This is an excellent way of cooking fish, leaving it moist in the middle and crisp and spicy on the outside.

SERVES 4

1 quantity Cajun spice mix, without the onion and garlic
4 x 225–275g/8–10oz fish fillets, such as snapper or bream, skinned
50g/2oz/¼ cup butter, melted
PAPAYA SALSA
1 papaya
½ small red onion, diced
1 fresh red chilli, seeded and finely chopped
45ml/3 tbsp chopped fresh coriander (cilantro)
grated rind and juice of 1 lime
lime and coriander (cilantro), to garnish

1 Start by making the salsa. Cut the papaya in half and scoop out the seeds. Remove the skin, cut the flesh into small dice and place it in a bowl. Add the onion, chilli, coriander, lime rind and juice, with salt to taste. Mix well and set aside.

COOK'S TIP

Cooking fish in this way can be a smoky affair, so make sure the kitchen is well ventilated or use an extractor fan.

---

2 Preheat a heavy frying pan over a medium heat for about 10 minutes. Spread the Cajun spice on a plate. Brush the fish fillets with melted butter then dip them in the spices until well coated.

3 Place the fish in the hot pan and cook for 1–2 minutes on each side until blackened. Serve immediately with the papaya salsa. Garnish with lime and coriander.

Caribbean Fish Steaks

West Indian cooks love spices and use them to good effect. This quick and easy recipe is a typical example of how chillies, cayenne and allspice can add an exotic accent to a tomato sauce for fish.

SERVES 4

45ml/3 tbsp oil
6 shallots, finely chopped
1 garlic clove, crushed
1 fresh green chilli, seeded and finely chopped
400g/14oz can chopped tomatoes
2 bay leaves
1.5ml/¼ tsp cayenne pepper
5ml/1 tsp crushed allspice
juice of 2 limes
4 cod steaks
5ml/1 tsp muscovado (molasses) sugar
10ml/2 tsp angostura bitters
salt

1 Heat the oil in a frying pan. Add the shallots and cook for 5 minutes until soft. Add the garlic and chilli and cook for 2 minutes, then stir in the tomatoes, bay leaves, cayenne pepper, allspice and lime juice, with a little salt to taste.

VARIATION

Almost any robust fish steaks or fillets can be cooked in this way. Try haddock or swordfish. The sauce is also good over grilled (broiled) pork chops.

---

2 Cook gently for 15 minutes, then add the cod steaks and baste with the tomato sauce. Cover and cook for 10 minutes or until the steaks are cooked. Transfer the steaks to a warmed dish and keep hot. Stir the sugar and angostura bitters into the sauce, simmer for 2 minutes, then pour over the fish. Serve with steamed okra or green beans.

Crab cakes with Ginger and Wasabi

Wasabi, Japanese horse-radish mustard, is available as a powder or a paste.

SERVES 6

450g/1lb fresh dressed crab meat (brown and white meat)

4 spring onions (scallions), finely chopped

2.5cm/1in piece of fresh root ginger, grated

30ml/2 tbsp chopped fresh coriander (cilantro)

30ml/2 tbsp mayonnaise

2.5–5ml/½–1 tsp wasabi paste

15ml/1 tbsp sesame oil

50–115g/2–4oz/1–2 cups fresh breadcrumbs

salt and ground black pepper

oil, for frying

DIPPING SAUCE

5ml/1 tsp wasabi paste

90ml/6 tbsp soy sauce

1 Make the dipping sauce by mixing the wasabi and soy sauce in a small bowl. Set aside.

2 Mix the crab meat, spring onions, ginger, coriander, mayonnaise, wasabi paste and sesame oil in a bowl. Stir in a little salt and pepper and enough breadcrumbs to make a mixture that is firm enough to form patties, but is not too stiff.

3 Chill for 30 minutes then form the mixture into 12 cakes. Heat a little oil in a frying pan and fry the crab cakes for about 3–4 minutes on each side, until browned. Serve with lettuce leaves and kaffir lime slices, accompanied by the dipping sauce, garnished with chilli and spring onion slices.

COOK'S TIP

Fresh crab meat will have the best flavour, but if it is not available, use frozen or canned crab meat.

Stir-fried Five Spice Squid with Black Bean Sauce

Squid is perfect for stir-frying as it should be cooked quickly. The spicy sauce makes the ideal accompaniment.

SERVES 6

450g/1lb small cleaned squid
45ml/3 tbsp oil
2.5cm/1in piece fresh root
 ginger, grated
1 garlic clove, crushed
8 spring onions (scallions), cut
 diagonally into 2.5cm/1in slices
1 red (bell) pepper, seeded and
 cut into strips
1 fresh green chilli, seeded and
 thinly sliced
6 mushrooms, sliced
5ml/1 tsp Chinese five-spice powder
30ml/2 tbsp black bean sauce
30ml/2 tbsp soy sauce
5ml/1 tsp granulated sugar
15ml/1 tbsp rice wine or dry sherry

COOK'S TIP

As with all stir-fried dishes it is important to have all the ingredients prepared before you start to cook.

1 Rinse the squid and pull away the outer skin. Dry on kitchen paper. Slit the squid open and score the outside into diamonds with a sharp knife. Cut the squid into strips.

2 Heat a wok briefly and add the oil. When it is hot, stir-fry the squid quickly. Remove the squid strips from the wok with a slotted spoon and set aside. Add the ginger, garlic, spring onions, red pepper, chilli and mushrooms to the oil remaining in the wok and stir-fry for 2 minutes.

3 Return the squid to the wok and stir in the five-spice powder. Stir in the black bean sauce, soy sauce, sugar and rice wine or sherry. Bring to the boil and cook, stirring, for 1 minute.

Cod and Prawn Green Coconut Curry

If you have a jar of green masala in the pantry, this curry takes just minutes to make!

SERVES 4

675g/1½lb cod fillets, skinned
90ml/6 tbsp green masala
175ml/6fl oz/¾ cup canned
   coconut milk
175g/6oz raw prawns
   (shrimp), peeled
fresh coriander (cilantro),
   to garnish
basmati rice, to serve

1 Cut the skinned cod fillets into 4cm/1½in pieces.

2 Put the green masala and coconut milk into a frying pan. Heat to simmering and simmer gently for 5 minutes, stirring occasionally.

VARIATION

Any firm fish, such as monkfish, can be used instead of cod. Whole fish steaks can be cooked in the sauce, but allow an extra 5 minutes' cooking time and baste them with the sauce from time to time.

3 Add the cod and prawns and cook for 5 minutes. Garnish with coriander and serve immediately with rice.

Piri-piri Prawns with Aioli

Piri-piri is a Portuguese hot pepper sauce. The name literally means a small chilli.

SERVES 4

1 red chilli, seeded and chopped
2.5ml/½ tsp paprika
2.5ml/½ tsp ground coriander
1 garlic clove, crushed
juice of ½ lime
30ml/2 tbsp olive oil
20 large raw prawns (jumbo
   shrimp) in shells, heads
   removed and deveined
salt and ground black pepper
AIOLI
150ml/¼ pint/⅔ cup mayonnaise
2 garlic cloves, crushed
5ml/1 tsp Dijon mustard
2–3 red chillies, to garnish

1 Make the aioli. Combine the mayonnaise, garlic and mustard in a small bowl and set aside.

VARIATION

The piri-piri marinade can be used for all types of fish. It is also very good with chicken, although this will need to be marinated for longer.

2 Mix the chilli, paprika, coriander, garlic, lime juice and olive oil in a bowl. Add salt and pepper to taste. Place the prawns in a dish. Add the spice mixture and mix well. Cover and leave in a cool place for 30 minutes.

3 Thread the prawns on to skewers and grill (broil) or cook on the barbecue, basting and turning frequently, for 6–8 minutes until pink. Serve with the aioli, garnished with 2–3 extra chillies, if you like.

Marrakesh Monkfish with Chermoula

Chermoula is a Moroccan spice mixture, which is used as a marinade for meat, poultry and fish.

SERVES 4

1 small red onion, finely chopped
2 garlic cloves, crushed
1 fresh red chilli, seeded and
  finely chopped
30ml/2 tbsp chopped fresh
  coriander (cilantro)
15ml/1 tbsp chopped fresh mint
5ml/1 tsp ground cumin
5ml/1 tsp paprika
generous pinch of
  saffron threads
60ml/4 tbsp olive oil
juice of 1 lemon
salt
675g/1½lb monkfish fillets
salad and pitta bread, to serve

1 To make the chermoula, mix the onion, garlic, chilli, coriander, mint, cumin, paprika, saffron, olive oil, lemon juice and salt in a bowl.

2 Skin the monkfish, if necessary, and cut it into cubes. Add them to the spice mixture. Mix well to coat, cover and leave in a cool place for 1 hour.

3 Thread the monkfish on to skewers and place on a grill (broiler) rack. Spoon over a little of the marinade.

4 Grill (broil) the monkfish skewers, close to the heat, for about 3 minutes on each side, until cooked through and lightly browned. Serve with salad and warm pitta bread.

> ### COOK'S TIP
>
> *If you use bamboo or wooden skewers, soak them in cold water for about 30 minutes before draining and threading them. This helps to prevent the skewers from scorching.*

Salmon Marinated with Thai Spices

This recipe takes a Scandinavian idea and transforms it with Thai spices.

SERVES 4–6

salmon tail piece, about 675g/
  1¹⁄₂lb, cleaned and prepared
20ml/4 tsp coarse sea salt
20ml/4 tsp granulated sugar
2.5cm/1in piece fresh root
  ginger, grated
2 lemon grass stalks, coarse
  outer leaves removed,
  thinly sliced
4 kaffir lime leaves,
  finely chopped or shredded
grated rind of 1 lime
1 fresh red chilli, seeded and
  finely chopped
5ml/1 tsp black peppercorns,
  coarsely crushed
30ml/2 tbsp chopped fresh
  coriander (cilantro)
coriander (cilantro) and kaffir
  limes, to garnish
CORIANDER AND LIME DIP
150ml/¹⁄₄ pint/²⁄₃ cup mayonnaise
juice of ¹⁄₂ lime
10ml/2 tsp chopped fresh
  coriander (cilantro)

1 Remove all the bones from the salmon (a pair of tweezers is the best tool). In a bowl, mix together the salt, sugar, ginger, lemon grass, lime leaves, lime rind, chilli, peppercorns and coriander.

2 Place one-quarter of the spice mixture in a shallow dish. Place one salmon fillet, skin-side down, on top of the spices. Spread two-thirds of the remaining mixture over the flesh, then place the remaining fillet on top, flesh-side down. Sprinkle the rest of the spice mixture over the fish.

COOK'S TIP

Ask your fishmonger to scale the fish, split it lengthwise and remove it from the backbone in two matching fillets.

3 Cover the fish with foil, then place a board on top. Add some weights, such as clean cans of fruit. Chill for 2–5 days, turning the fish daily in the spicy brine.

4 Make the dip by mixing the mayonnaise, lime juice and chopped coriander in a bowl.

5 Scrape the spices off the fish. Slice it as thinly as possible. Garnish with coriander and wedges of kaffir limes and serve with the lime dip.

POULTRY AND GAME

Moroccan Harissa-spiced Roast Chicken

The spices and fruit in this stuffing give the chicken an unusual flavour and help to keep it moist.

SERVES 4–5

1.3–1.6kg/3–3½lb chicken
30–60ml/2–4 tbsp garlic and spice
  aromatic oil
a few bay leaves
10ml/2 tsp clear honey
10ml/2 tsp tomato purée (paste)
60ml/4 tbsp lemon juice
150ml/¼ pint/⅔ cup
  chicken stock
2.5–5ml/½–1 tsp harissa
STUFFING
25g/1oz/2 tbsp butter
1 onion, chopped
1 garlic clove, crushed
7.5ml/1½ tsp ground cinnamon
2.5ml/½ tsp ground cumin
225g/8oz/1⅓ cups dried fruit,
  soaked for several hours or
  overnight in water to cover
25g/1oz/¼ cup blanched almonds,
  finely chopped
salt and ground black pepper

COOK'S TIP

If you do not particularly like mixed dried fruit, use a single variety, such as apricots, instead.

1 Make the stuffing. Melt the butter in a pan. Add the onion and garlic and cook over a low heat for 5 minutes until soft. Add the ground cinnamon and cumin and cook, stirring constantly, for 2 minutes.

2 Drain the dried fruit, chop it roughly and add to the stuffing with the almonds. Season with salt and pepper and cook for 2 minutes more. Tip into a bowl and leave to cool.

3 Preheat the oven to 200°C/400°F/ Gas 6. Stuff the neck of the chicken with the fruit mixture, reserving any excess. Brush the garlic and spice oil over the chicken. Place the chicken in a roasting pan, tuck in the bay leaves and roast for 1–1¼ hours, basting occasionally with the pan juices, until cooked.

4 Transfer the chicken to a carving board. Pour off any excess fat from the roasting pan. Stir the honey, tomato purée, lemon juice, stock and harissa into the juices in the roasting pan. Add salt to taste. Bring to the boil, lower the heat and simmer for 2 minutes, stirring frequently. Meanwhile, reheat any excess stuffing. Carve the chicken, pour the sauce into a small bowl and serve with the stuffing and chicken.

Fragrant Chicken Curry with Thai Spices

This is perfect for a party as the chicken and sauce can be prepared in advance and combined at the last minute.

SERVES 4

45ml/3 tbsp oil
1 onion, roughly chopped
2 garlic cloves, crushed
15ml/1 tbsp Thai red curry paste
115g/4oz creamed coconut
   (coconut cream) dissolved
   in 900ml/1½ pints/3¾ cups
   boiling water
2 lemon grass stalks, chopped
6 kaffir lime leaves, chopped
150ml/¼ pint/⅔ cup Greek
   (US strained, plain) yogurt
30ml/2 tbsp apricot jam
1 cooked chicken, 1.3–1.6kg/3–3½lb
30ml/2 tbsp chopped fresh
   coriander (cilantro)
salt and ground black pepper
kaffir limes leaves, shredded
   coconut and fresh coriander,
   (cilantro) to garnish
plain boiled rice, to serve

1 Heat the oil in a pan. Fry the onion and garlic gently for 5–10 minutes until soft. Stir in the curry paste. Cook, stirring constantly, for 2–3 minutes. Stir in the diluted creamed coconut, then add the lemon grass, lime leaves, yogurt and apricot jam. Stir well. Cover and simmer for 30 minutes.

2 Process the sauce in a blender or food processor, then strain it back into a clean pan, pressing as much of the puréed mixture as possible through the sieve.

3 Remove the skin from the chicken, slice the meat off the bones and cut it into bitesize pieces. Add to the sauce.

4 Bring the sauce back to simmering point. Stir in the fresh coriander and season with salt and pepper. Serve with rice, garnished with extra lime leaves, shredded coconut and coriander.

COOK'S TIP

If you prefer the sauce thicker, stir in a little more creamed coconut after adding the chicken.

Turkey Sosaties with a Curried Apricot Sauce

This is a South African way of cooking meat or poultry in a delicious sweet and sour sauce spiced with curry powder.

SERVES 4

15ml/1 tbsp oil
1 onion, finely chopped
1 garlic clove, crushed
2 bay leaves
juice of 1 lemon
30ml/2 tbsp curry powder
60ml/4 tbsp apricot jam
60ml/4 tbsp apple juice
salt
675g/1½lb turkey fillet
60ml/4 tbsp crème fraîche

1 Heat the oil in a pan. Add the onion, garlic and bay leaves and cook over a low heat for 10 minutes until the onions are soft. Add the lemon juice, curry powder, apricot jam and apple juice, with salt to taste. Cook gently for 5 minutes. Leave to cool.

VARIATION

This marinade is traditionally used with lamb, and is equally good with cubes of pork fillet (tenderloin) or chicken.

2 Cut the turkey into 2cm/¾in cubes and add to the marinade. Mix well, cover and leave in a cool place to marinate for at least 2 hours or overnight in the refrigerator. Thread the turkey on to skewers, allowing the marinade to run back into the bowl. Grill (broil) or cook on the barbecue for 6–8 minutes, turning several times.

3 Meanwhile, transfer the marinade to a pan and simmer for 2 minutes. Stir in the crème fraîche and serve with the sosaties.

Spicy Indonesian Chicken Satay

This spicy marinade quickly gives an exotic flavour to tender chicken. The satays can be cooked on a barbecue or under the grill.

SERVES 4

4 skinless, boneless chicken
  breast portions, 175g/6oz each
1 quantity sambal kecap, with
  the deep-fried onions separate

1 Cut the chicken breast portions into 2.5cm/1in cubes and place in a bowl with the sambal kecap. Mix thoroughly. Cover and leave in a cool place to marinate for at least 1 hour. Soak 8 bamboo skewers in cold water for 30 minutes.

2 Tip the chicken and marinade into a sieve placed over a pan and leave to drain for a few minutes. Set the sieve and chicken aside.

3 Add 30ml/2 tbsp hot water to the marinade and bring to the boil. Lower the heat and simmer for 2 minutes. Pour into a bowl and leave to cool. When cool, add the deep-fried onions.

4 Drain the skewers, thread them with the chicken and grill (broil) or cook on the barbecue for about 10 minutes, turning regularly until the chicken is golden brown and cooked through. Serve immediately with the sambal kecap as a dip.

Spiced Poussins

The cumin and coriander coating on the poussins keeps them moist during cooking as well as giving them a delicious and unusual flavour.

SERVES 4

2 garlic cloves, coarsely chopped
5ml/1 tsp ground cumin
5ml/1 tsp ground coriander
pinch of cayenne pepper
½ small onion, chopped
60ml/4 tbsp olive oil
2.5ml/½ tsp salt
2 poussins
lemon wedges, to garnish

1 Combine the garlic, cumin, coriander, cayenne pepper, onion, olive oil and salt in a blender or food processor. Process to make a paste that will spread smoothly.

VARIATION

Chicken portions and quail can also be cooked in this way.

2 Cut the poussins in half lengthwise. Place them skin-side up in a shallow dish and spread with the spice paste. Cover and leave to marinate in a cool place for 2 hours.

3 Grill (broil) or cook on the barbecue for 15–20 minutes, turning frequently, until cooked and lightly charred. Serve immediately, garnished with lemon wedges.

Chicken with Forty Cloves of Garlic

This recipe is not so alarming as it sounds. Long slow cooking makes the garlic soft and fragrant and the delicious flavour permeates the chicken.

SERVES 4–6

½ lemon
fresh rosemary sprigs
1.3–2kg/3–4½lb chicken
4–5 heads of garlic
60ml/4 tbsp olive oil
salt and ground black pepper
steamed broad (fava) beans and
  spring onions (scallions),
  to serve

1 Preheat the oven to 190°C/375°F/ Gas 5. Place the lemon half and the rosemary sprigs in the chicken. Separate 3–4 of the garlic heads into cloves and remove the papery husks, but do not peel. Slice the top off the other garlic head.

COOK'S TIP

Make sure that each guest receives an equal portion of garlic. The idea is to mash the garlic into the pan juices to make an aromatic sauce.

2 Heat the oil in a large flameproof casserole. Add the chicken, turning it in the hot oil to coat the skin completely. Season with salt and pepper and add all the garlic.

3 Cover the casserole with a sheet of foil, then the lid to seal in the steam and the flavour. Cook in the oven for 1–1¼ hours until the chicken is cooked. Serve the chicken with the garlic, accompanied by steamed broad beans and spring onions.

Mediterranean Duck with Harissa and Saffron

Harissa is a fiery chilli sauce from North Africa. Mixed with cinnamon, saffron and preserved lemon, it gives this colourful casserole an unforgettable flavour.

SERVES 4

15ml/1 tbsp olive oil
1.8–2kg/4–4½ lb duck, quartered
1 large onion, thinly sliced
1 garlic clove, crushed
2.5ml/½ tsp ground cumin
400ml/14fl oz/1⅔ cups duck or
  chicken stock
juice of ½ lemon
5–10ml/1–2 tsp harissa
1 cinnamon stick
5ml/1 tsp saffron threads
50g/2oz/½ cup pitted black olives
50g/2oz/½ cup pitted green olives
peel of 1 preserved lemon, rinsed,
  drained and cut into strips
2–3 lemon slices
30ml/2 tbsp chopped fresh
  coriander (cilantro)
salt and ground black pepper
coriander sprigs, to garnish

1 Heat the olive oil in a flameproof casserole. Add the duck quarters and cook until browned all over. Remove with a slotted spoon and set aside. Add the onion and garlic to the oil remaining in the casserole and cook for 5 minutes until soft. Add the cumin and cook, stirring, for 2 minutes.

2 Pour in the stock and lemon juice, then add the harissa, cinnamon and saffron. Bring to the boil. Return the duck to the casserole and add the olives, preserved lemon peel and lemon slices. Season with salt and pepper.

3 Lower the heat, partially cover the casserole and simmer gently for 45 minutes until the duck is cooked through. Discard the cinnamon stick. Stir in the chopped coriander and garnish with the coriander sprigs.

Tea-smoked Duck Breasts

Steaming spiced duck breast over fragrant tea leaves gives it a slightly smoky flavour, which is not too overpowering.

SERVES 2–4

2 duck breast portions
60ml/4 tbsp Seven-seas curry powder
15ml/1 tbsp soy sauce
115g/4oz/½ cup long grain rice
115g/4oz/½ cup granulated sugar
30ml/2 tbsp Earl Grey tea leaves
stir-fried pak choi (bok choy), to serve

VARIATION

Whole chicken and duck, chicken portions, quail and other game or fish steaks can be smoked in the same way. Fish does not need to be steamed first. A whole bird will take about 1 hour.

1 Pat the duck dry with kitchen paper. Rub the curry powder all over the meat. Pour water into a wok to the depth of 5–7.5cm/2–3in.

2 Place the duck on a steaming rack over the water. Cover the wok and steam the duck for 20–30 minutes, depending on the thickness of the meat. Remove the duck and sprinkle with soy sauce. Set aside.

3 Wash and dry the wok and line with two sheets of foil. Mix together the raw rice, sugar and tea. Spread the mixture in the bottom of the lined wok. Place the duck breast portions on the steaming rack above the tea mixture. Put the lid on and seal the rim with damp kitchen paper.

4 Place the wok over a medium heat. As soon as you can smell that it has started smoking leave it, undisturbed, for 10–15 minutes. Remove from the heat, and leave, covered, for a further 15 minutes. Discard the rice. Cut the duck into thin slices and serve warm or cold with pak choi.

Roast Rabbit with Three Mustards

In France, rabbit and mustard are a popular combination. In this recipe each of the three different mustards adds a distinctive flavour to the dish.

SERVES 4

15ml/1 tbsp Dijon mustard
15ml/1 tbsp tarragon mustard
15ml/1 tbsp wholegrain mustard
1.3–1.6kg/3–3½lb rabbit portions
1 large carrot, sliced
1 onion, sliced
30ml/2 tbsp chopped fresh
  tarragon
120ml/4fl oz/½ cup dry
  white wine
150ml/¼ pint/⅔ cup
  double (heavy) cream
salt and ground black pepper
chopped fresh tarragon, to garnish

VARIATION

If the three different mustards are not available, use one or two varieties, increasing the quantities accordingly. The flavour will not be quite so interesting, but the dish will still taste good!

1 Preheat the oven to 200°C/400°F/ Gas 6. Mix the mustards in a bowl and spread over the rabbit. Put the carrot and onion slices in a roasting pan and sprinkle the tarragon over. Pour in 120ml/4fl oz/½ cup of water, then arrange the meat on top.

2 Roast for 25–30 minutes, basting frequently with the juices, until the rabbit is tender. Remove the rabbit to a heated serving dish and keep hot. Using a slotted spoon, remove the carrot and onion slices from the roasting pan and discard.

3 Place the roasting pan on the hob (stovetop) and add the white wine. Boil to reduce by about two-thirds. Stir in the cream and allow to bubble up for a few minutes. Season with salt and pepper then pour over the rabbit and serve, garnished with fresh tarragon.

Venison in Guinness with Horseradish and Mustard Dumplings

Mustard, juniper berries and bay leaves combine with lean dark venison to create a casserole with a rich flavour and wonderful aroma.

SERVES 6

15ml/1 tbsp olive oil
675g/1½lb stewing venison,
 cut into cubes
3 onions, sliced
2 garlic cloves, crushed
15ml/1 tbsp plain (all-purpose) flour
5ml/1 tsp mustard powder
6 juniper berries, lightly crushed
2 bay leaves
400ml/14fl oz/1⅔ cups Guinness
10ml/2 tsp light brown sugar
30ml/2 tbsp balsamic vinegar
salt and ground black pepper

DUMPLINGS

175g/6oz/1½ cups self-raising
 (self-rising) flour
5ml/1 tsp mustard powder
75g/3oz/generous ½ cup
 shredded beef suet
10ml/2 tsp horseradish sauce

1 Preheat the oven to 180°C/350°F/ Gas 4. Heat the oil in a flameproof casserole. Fry the meat, a few pieces at a time, until browned. As each batch browns, remove it to a plate. Add the onions, with a little more oil, if necessary. Cook, stirring, for 5 minutes until soft. Add the garlic, then return the venison to the casserole.

2 Mix the flour and mustard in a small bowl, sprinkle over the venison and stir well until the flour has been absorbed. Add the juniper berries and bay leaves and gradually stir in the Guinness, sugar and vinegar. Pour over enough water to cover the meat. Season with salt and pepper and bring to simmering point.

3 Cover and transfer the casserole to cook in the oven for 2–2½ hours, until the venison is tender. Stir the casserole occasionally and add a little more water, if necessary.

4 About 20 minutes before the end of the cooking time, make the dumplings. Sift the flour and mustard into a bowl. Season with salt and pepper and mix in the suet. Stir in the horseradish sauce and enough water to make a soft dough. With floured hands, form into 6 dumplings. Place these on top of the venison. Return the casserole to the oven and cook for 15 minutes more, until the dumplings are well risen and cooked. Serve immediately.

BEEF, LAMB AND PORK

Beef Teriyaki

Mirin is a sweetened sake, widely used in Japanese cooking. However, it is hard to find outside of Japanese grocers, so a medium-sweet sherry can be used instead. Sansho pepper is a ground Japanese spice, used to counter fatty flavours.

SERVES 4

15ml/1 tbsp oil
60ml/4 tbsp soy sauce
30ml/2 tbsp mirin or sherry
5ml/1 tsp light brown sugar
15ml/1 tbsp ginger juice
1 garlic clove, crushed
675–900g/1½–2lb rump (round) steak, about 2.5cm/1in thick
sansho pepper
1 mooli (daikon), peeled, to garnish
30ml/2 tbsp wasabi paste, to serve
fresh coriander (cilantro) sprigs, to garnish

1 Mix the oil, soy sauce, mirin or sherry, sugar, ginger juice and garlic in a large shallow dish. Add the steak and turn to coat both sides. Leave in a cool place to marinate for at least 4 hours, turning from time to time.

2 Preheat a grill (broiler), ridged cast iron griddle pan or barbecue and cook the steak for 3–5 minutes on each side. Season with sansho pepper.

3 To prepare the Japanese-style garnish, grate the mooli and squeeze out as much liquid as possible. Place a little pile of grated mooli, a dessertspoonful of wasabi paste and a coriander sprig on each of 4 plates.

4 With a sharp knife, slice the steak into thin diagonal slices and arrange on the plates with the garnish.

COOK'S TIP

To make ginger juice, peel and grate a piece of root ginger and squeeze out the liquid.

Black Bean Chilli con Carne

Two chillies add plenty of fire to this Tex-Mex classic.

SERVES 6

225g/8oz/1¼ cups dried
  black beans
500g/1¼lb braising steak
30ml/2 tbsp oil
2 onions, chopped
1 garlic clove, crushed
1 fresh green chilli, seeded and
  finely chopped
15ml/1 tbsp paprika
10ml/2 tsp ground cumin
10ml/2 tsp ground coriander
400g/14oz can chopped tomatoes
300ml/½ pint/1¼ cups beef stock
1 dried red chilli, crumbled
5ml/1 tsp hot pepper sauce
1 fresh red (bell) pepper, seeded
  and diced
salt
30ml/2 tbsp fresh coriander
  (cilantro) leaves, to garnish
plain boiled rice, to serve

1 Put the beans in a pan. Add water to cover, bring to the boil and boil vigorously for 10–15 minutes. Drain, tip into a clean bowl, cover with cold water and leave to soak for about 8 hours or overnight.

2 Preheat the oven to 150°C/300°F/ Gas 2. Cut the beef into very small dice. Heat the oil in a large flameproof casserole. Add the onion, garlic and green chilli and cook them gently for 5 minutes until soft. Using a slotted spoon, transfer the mixture to a plate.

3 Increase the heat and brown the meat, then stir in the paprika, cumin and ground coriander.

4 Add the tomatoes, stock, dried chilli and pepper sauce. Drain the beans and add them to the casserole, with enough water to cover them. Bring the water to simmering point, cover and cook in the oven for 2 hours. Stir the casserole occasionally and add extra water, if necessary, to prevent it from drying out.

5 Season with salt and add the red pepper. Return to the oven and cook for 30 minutes more, until the meat and beans are tender. Sprinkle over the coriander and serve with rice.

Roast Lamb with Apricot, Cinnamon and Cumin Stuffing

Cinnamon and cumin make perfect partners for apricots in the bulgur wheat stuffing in this easy-to-carve joint.

SERVES 6–8

75g/3oz/½ cup bulgur wheat
30ml/2 tbsp olive oil
1 small onion, finely chopped
1 garlic clove, crushed
5ml/1 tsp ground cinnamon
5ml/1 tsp ground cumin
175g/6oz/¾ cup ready-to-eat dried
  apricots, chopped
50g/2oz/⅔ cup pine nuts
1 boned shoulder of lamb, about
  1.8–2kg/4–4½lb
120ml/4fl oz/½ cup red wine
120ml/4fl oz/½ cup lamb stock
salt and ground black pepper
mint sprigs, to garnish

1 Place the bulgur wheat in a bowl and add warm water to cover. Leave to soak for 1 hour, then drain thoroughly.

2 Heat the oil in a pan. Add the onion and crushed garlic and cook for 5 minutes until soft. Stir in the cinnamon, cumin, apricots and pine nuts, with salt and pepper to taste. Leave to cool. Preheat the oven to 180°C/350°F/Gas 4.

3 Open out the shoulder of lamb and spread the stuffing over. Roll up firmly and tie tightly with string. Place in a roasting pan. Roast for 1 hour, then pour the red wine and stock into the roasting pan. Roast for 30 minutes more. Transfer the lamb to a heated plate, cover with tented foil and allow the meat to rest for 15–20 minutes before carving.

4 Meanwhile, skim the surface fat from the wine-flavoured stock in the roasting pan. Place the pan over a high heat and allow the gravy to bubble for a few minutes, stirring occasionally to incorporate any sediment. Carve the lamb neatly, arrange the slices on a serving platter and pour over the gravy. Serve immediately, garnished with mint sprigs.

Green Peppercorn and Cinnamon Crusted Lamb

Racks of lamb are perfect for serving at dinner parties. This version has a delicious spiced crumb coating.

SERVES 6

50g/2oz ciabatta bread
15ml/1 tbsp drained green peppercorns in brine, lightly crushed
15ml/1 tbsp ground cinnamon
1 garlic clove, crushed
2.5ml/½ tsp salt
25g/1oz/2 tbsp butter, melted
10ml/2 tsp Dijon mustard
2 racks of lamb, trimmed
60ml/4 tbsp red wine
400ml/14fl oz/1⅔ cups lamb stock
15ml/1 tbsp balsamic vinegar
peas and baby carrots, to serve

VARIATION

The spicy crumbs also make a tasty coating for chicken pieces, fish or chops.

1 Preheat the oven to 220°C/425°F/ Gas 7. Break the ciabatta into pieces, spread out on a baking sheet and bake for 10 minutes or until pale golden. Process in a blender or food processor to make crumbs.

2 Tip the crumbs into a bowl and add the green peppercorns, cinnamon, garlic and salt. Stir in the melted butter. Spread the mustard over the lamb. Press the crumb mixture on to the mustard to make a thin even crust. Put the racks in a roasting pan and roast for 30 minutes, covering the ends with foil if they start to over-brown.

3 Remove the lamb to a carving dish and keep hot under tented foil. Skim the fat off the juices in the roasting pan. Stir in the wine, stock and vinegar. Bring to the boil, stirring any sediment, then lower the heat and simmer for about 10 minutes until reduced to a rich gravy. Carve the lamb. Serve with the gravy and vegetables.

Lamb Tagine

Combining meat, dried fruit and spices is typical of Middle Eastern cooking. This type of casserole takes its name from the earthenware pot (tagine) in which it is traditionally cooked.

SERVES 4–6

115g/4oz/½ cup dried apricots
30ml/2 tbsp olive oil
1 large onion, chopped
1kg/2¼lb boneless shoulder of lamb, cubed
5ml/1 tsp ground cumin
5ml/1 tsp ground coriander
5ml/1 tsp ground cinnamon
grated rind and juice of ½ orange
5ml/1 tsp saffron threads
15ml/1 tbsp ground almonds
about 300ml/½ pint/1¼ cups lamb or chicken stock
15ml/1 tbsp sesame seeds
salt and ground black pepper
fresh flat-leaf parsley, to garnish
couscous, to serve

COOK'S TIP

If you do not have time to soak the apricots, use the ready-to-eat variety and add extra stock to replace the soaking liquid.

1 Cut the apricots in half and put in a bowl with 150ml/¼ pint/⅔ cup water. Leave to soak overnight.

2 Preheat the oven to 180°C/350°F/ Gas 4. Heat the olive oil in a flameproof casserole. Add the onion and cook gently for 10 minutes until soft and golden.

3 Stir in the lamb. Add the cumin, coriander and cinnamon, with salt and pepper to taste. Stir to coat the lamb cubes in the spices. Cook, stirring constantly, for 5 minutes.

4 Add the apricots and their soaking liquid. Stir in the orange rind and juice, saffron, almonds and enough stock to cover. Cover the casserole and cook in the oven for 1–1½ hours until the meat is tender, stirring occasionally and adding extra stock, if necessary.

5 Heat a heavy frying pan, add the sesame seeds and dry-fry, shaking the pan, until golden. Sprinkle the sesame seeds over the meat, garnish with parsley and serve with couscous.

Turkish Kebabs with Tomato and Olive Salsa

The mix of aromatic spices, garlic and lemon give these kebabs a wonderful flavour and a fiery salsa makes the perfect accompaniment.

SERVES 4

2 garlic cloves, crushed
60ml/4 tbsp lemon juice
30ml/2 tbsp olive oil
1 dried red chilli, crushed
5ml/1 tsp ground cumin
5ml/1 tsp ground coriander
500g/1¼lb lean lamb, cut into
   4cm/1½in cubes
8 bay leaves
salt and ground black pepper

TOMATO AND OLIVE SALSA

175g/6oz/1½ cups mixed pitted
   green and black olives,
   coarsely chopped
1 small red onion, finely chopped
4 plum tomatoes, peeled and
   finely chopped
1 fresh red chilli, seeded and
   finely chopped
30ml/2 tbsp olive oil

1 Mix the garlic, lemon juice, olive oil, chilli, cumin and coriander in a large shallow dish. Add the lamb cubes, with salt and pepper to taste. Mix well. Cover and marinate in a cool place for 2 hours.

2 Make the salsa. Put the olives, onion, tomatoes, chilli and olive oil in a bowl. Season with salt and pepper to taste. Mix well, cover and set aside.

3 Remove the lamb from the marinade and divide the cubes among 4 skewers, adding the bay leaves at intervals. Cook over a barbecue, on a ridged iron griddle pan or under a hot grill (broiler), turning occasionally, for 10 minutes, until the lamb is browned on the outside and pink and juicy inside. Serve with the salsa.

Veal Escalopes with Ruby Grapefruit and Ginger

The ginger and pink peppercorns give the grapefruit sauce a subtle spiciness without being overpowering.

SERVES 4

4 veal escalopes (scallops)
25g/1oz/2 tbsp butter
15ml/1 tbsp olive oil
juice of 1 large ruby grapefruit
150ml/¼ pint/⅔ cup chicken stock
10ml/2 tsp grated fresh root ginger
5ml/1 tsp pink peppercorns, drained and lightly crushed
15g/½oz/1 tbsp cold butter
salt
GARNISH
1 ruby grapefruit
oil, for shallow frying

1 Start by making the garnish. Wash and dry the grapefruit, then pare off thin strips of rind, using a citrus zester. Scrape off any pith that remains attached to the strips. Cut the grapefruit in half. Squeeze the juice from half the grapefruit into a small bowl, add the strips of pared rind and leave to macerate for 1 hour. Cut the other half into wedges and reserve.

2 Drain the strips of rind and pat them dry with kitchen paper. Heat the oil to a depth of 1cm/½in in a small pan and add the strips. As soon as they are brown, strain the strips through a sieve into a bowl, then discard the oil.

3 Place the veal escalopes between 2 sheets of baking parchment and beat them with a rolling pin until they are about 3mm/⅛in thick. If the escalopes are very large, cut them into neat pieces.

4 Melt the butter and the oil in a heavy frying pan. Fry the veal, in batches if necessary, for 1 minute on each side. Remove the escalopes to a heated dish and keep hot.

5 Add the grapefruit juice, stock and grated ginger to the pan. Allow to boil until reduced by half. Strain the sauce into a pan, add the peppercorns and heat through. Whisk in the cold butter and season with salt. Pour the sauce over the veal, then garnish with fried grapefruit rind and reserved wedges.

Tsire Koftas with Avocado and Melon Salsa

Tsire powder makes a lovely crunchy coating for the meat on these kebabs.

SERVES 4–6

675g/1½lb lean minced (ground) lamb
30ml/2 tbsp Greek (US strained, plain) yogurt
1 small onion, finely chopped
1 garlic clove, crushed
1.5ml/¼ tsp chilli powder
1 egg, beaten
double quantity tsire powder
salt and ground black pepper
mint leaves, to garnish

SALSA

1 ripe avocado
juice of 1 lime
225g/8oz melon, peeled, seeded and cut into small dice
4 spring onions (scallions), very finely chopped
1 fresh red chilli, seeded and finely chopped

1 Make the salsa. Cut the avocado in half, remove the stone (pit) and peel off the skin. Dice the flesh finely and toss it with the lime juice in a bowl. Add the melon, spring onions and chilli, with salt and pepper to taste. Cover and leave to stand for 30 minutes.

2 Put the minced lamb in a food processor with the yogurt, onion, garlic and chilli powder. Add a little salt and pepper and process until smooth.

3 Divide the lamb mixture into 12 portions and shape each one into a sausage shape. Push a pre-soaked bamboo skewer into each kofta and press the meat on to the stick.

4 Dip each kofta in egg, then roll it in the tsire powder. Cook over a barbecue or under a hot grill (broiler) for 10 minutes, turning occasionally until cooked. Serve with the salsa, garnished with mint leaves.

Paprika Pork with Fennel and Caraway

Fennel always tastes very good with pork, and combined with caraway seeds adds an aromatic flavour to this Central European dish.

SERVES 4

15ml/1 tbsp olive oil
4 boneless pork steaks
1 large onion, thinly sliced
400g/14oz can chopped tomatoes
5ml/1 tsp fennel seeds,
 lightly crushed
2.5ml/$\frac{1}{2}$ tsp caraway seeds,
 lightly crushed
15ml/1 tbsp paprika
30ml/2 tbsp sour cream
salt and ground black pepper
paprika, to garnish
buttered noodles and poppy
 seeds, to serve

COOK'S TIP

Always buy good quality paprika and replace it regularly, as it loses its distinctive flavour very quickly.

1 Heat the oil in a large frying pan. Add the pork steaks and brown on both sides. Lift out the steaks and put them on a plate.

2 Add the onion to the oil remaining in the pan. Cook for 10 minutes, until soft and golden. Stir in the tomatoes, fennel, caraway seeds and paprika.

3 Return the pork to the pan and simmer gently for 20–30 minutes until tender. Season with salt and pepper. Lightly swirl in the sour cream and sprinkle with a little paprika. Serve with noodles, tossed in butter and sprinkled with poppy seeds.

Baked Maple Ribs

The only way to eat these spicy ribs is with your fingers. So provide plenty of paper napkins!

SERVES 6

30ml/2 tbsp oil
1 onion, cut into thin wedges
1 garlic clove, crushed
105ml/7 tbsp maple syrup
15ml/1 tbsp soy sauce
15ml/1 tbsp tomato ketchup
15ml/1 tbsp Worcestershire sauce
5ml/1 tsp ground ginger
5ml/1 tsp paprika
5ml/1 tsp mustard powder
15ml/1 tbsp red wine vinegar
5ml/1 tsp Tabasco sauce
1kg/2¼ lb pork spare ribs

1 Preheat the oven to 200°C/400°F/ Gas 6. Heat the oil in a pan, add the onion and garlic and cook for about 5 minutes until soft.

2 Add the maple syrup, soy sauce, tomato ketchup, Worcestershire sauce, ginger, paprika, mustard powder, wine vinegar and Tabasco sauce. Bring to the boil, lower the heat and simmer for 2 minutes.

3 Place the ribs in a roasting pan, pour over the sauce and turn the ribs to coat completely. Cover the pan with foil and bake for 45 minutes. Remove the foil and bake for 15 minutes more, basting them occasionally. The ribs should be sticky and tender.

COOK'S TIP

Make sure you use real maple syrup and not maple-flavoured syrup for this recipe.

Jerk Pork

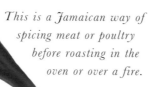

This is a Jamaican way of spicing meat or poultry before roasting in the oven or over a fire.

SERVES 4

15ml/1 tbsp oil
2 onions, finely chopped
2 fresh red chillies, seeded and
 finely chopped
1 garlic clove, crushed
2.5cm/1in piece of fresh root
 ginger, grated
5ml/1 tsp dried thyme
5ml/1 tsp ground allspice
5ml/1 tsp hot pepper sauce
30ml/2 tbsp rum
grated rind and juice of 1 lime
salt and ground black pepper
4 pork chops
fresh thyme, small red chillies
 and lime wedges, to garnish

1 Heat the oil in a frying pan. Add the onions and cook for 10 minutes until soft. Add the chillies, garlic, ginger, thyme and allspice and fry for 2 more minutes. Stir in the hot pepper sauce, rum, lime rind and juice.

VARIATION

Chicken pieces or a whole chicken can also be coated with this delicious spicy paste before roasting.

2 Simmer until the mixture forms a dark paste. Season with salt and pepper and leave to cool. Rub the paste over the chops. Put them in a shallow dish, cover and chill overnight.

3 Preheat the oven to 190°C/375°F/ Gas 5. Place the chops on a rack in a roasting pan and roast for 30 minutes until fully cooked. Serve immediately, garnished with fresh thyme, chillies and lime wedges.

VEGETABLES AND SALADS

Vegetable Korma

The blending of spices is an ancient art in India. Here the aim is to produce a subtle, aromatic curry rather than an assault on the senses.

SERVES 4

50g/2oz/¼ cup butter
2 onions, sliced
2 garlic cloves, crushed
2.5cm/1in piece fresh root
  ginger, grated
5ml/1 tsp ground cumin
15ml/1 tbsp ground coriander
6 cardamoms
5cm/2in cinnamon stick
5ml/1 tsp ground turmeric
1 fresh red chilli, seeded and
  finely chopped
1 small aubergine (eggplant)
115g/4oz/1½ cups mushrooms
1 potato, peeled and cut into
  2.5cm/1in cubes
115g/4oz/1 cup green beans
60ml/4 tbsp natural (plain) yogurt
150ml/¼ pint/⅔ cup
  double (heavy) cream
5ml/1 tsp garam masala
salt and ground black pepper
fresh coriander (cilantro) sprigs,
  to garnish
poppadums, to serve

1 Melt the butter in a heavy pan. Add the onions and cook for 5 minutes until soft. Add the garlic and ginger and cook for 2 minutes, then stir in the cumin, coriander, cardamoms, cinnamon stick, turmeric and chilli. Cook, stirring for 30 seconds.

2 Chop the aubergine and slice the mushrooms thickly. Add with the potato and about 175ml/6fl oz/¾ cup water. Cover the pan, bring to the boil, then lower the heat and simmer for 15 minutes. Add the beans and cook, uncovered, for 5 minutes.

VARIATION

Any combination of vegetables can be used for this korma, including carrots, cauliflower, broccoli, peas and chickpeas.

3 With a slotted spoon, remove the vegetables to a warmed serving dish and keep hot. Allow the cooking liquid to bubble up until it reduces a little. Season with salt and pepper, then stir in the yogurt, cream and garam masala. Pour the sauce over the vegetables and garnish with coriander. Serve with poppadums.

Dhal with Tadka

Boost your pulse rate with this delectable dish of red lentils with a spicy topping.

SERVES 4

50g/2oz/¼ cup butter

10ml/2 tsp black mustard seeds

1 onion, finely chopped

2 garlic cloves, finely chopped

5ml/1 tsp ground turmeric

5ml/1 tsp ground cumin

2 fresh green chillies, seeded and finely chopped

225g/8oz/1 cup red lentils

300ml/½ pint/1¼ cups canned coconut milk

1 quantity tadka

fresh coriander (cilantro), to garnish

1 Melt the butter in a large heavy pan over a low heat. Add the mustard seeds. When they start to pop, add the onion and garlic and cook for 5–10 minutes until soft.

2 Stir in the turmeric, cumin and chillies and cook for 2 minutes. Stir in the lentils, 1 litre/1¾ pints/4 cups water and the coconut milk. Bring to the boil, cover and simmer for 40 minutes, adding water if needed. The lentils should be soft and should have absorbed most of the liquid.

3 Prepare the tadka and pour immediately over the lentil mixture. Garnish with coriander leaves and serve at once, as part of an Indian meal, or on its own with naan bread to mop up the sauce.

VARIATION

This dish is excellent made with moong dhal, the yellow split mung bean that is widely used in Indian cooking.

Glazed Sweet Potatoes with Ginger and Allspice

Fried sweet potatoes acquire a candied coating when cooked with ginger, syrup and allspice. Cayenne cuts through the sweetness.

SERVES 4

900g/2lb sweet potatoes
50g/2oz/¼ cup butter
45ml/3 tbsp oil
2 garlic cloves, crushed
2 pieces of stem (crystallized) ginger, finely chopped
10ml/2 tsp ground allspice
15ml/1 tbsp syrup from ginger jar
salt and cayenne pepper
10ml/2 tsp chopped fresh thyme, plus a few sprigs to garnish

1 Peel the sweet potatoes and cut into 1cm/½in cubes. Melt the butter with the oil in a large frying pan. Add the sweet potato cubes and fry, stirring frequently, for about 10 minutes until they are just soft.

COOK'S TIP

Some sweet potatoes have white flesh and some have yellow. Although they taste similar, the yellow-fleshed variety look particularly colourful and attractive.

2 Stir in the garlic, ginger and allspice. Cook, stirring, for 5 minutes more. Stir in the ginger syrup, salt, a generous pinch of cayenne pepper and the fresh thyme. Stir for 1–2 minutes more, then serve sprinkled with thyme sprigs.

Roasted Root Vegetables with Whole Spice Seeds

Roast these vegetables alongside a joint or whole chicken and they virtually look after themselves.

SERVES 4

3 parsnips, peeled
3 potatoes, peeled
3 carrots, peeled
3 sweet potatoes, peeled
60ml/4 tbsp olive oil
8 shallots, peeled
2 garlic cloves, sliced
10ml/2 tsp white mustard seeds
10ml/2 tsp coriander seeds, lightly crushed
5ml/1 tsp cumin seeds
2 bay leaves
salt and ground black pepper

1 Preheat the oven to 190°C/375°F/ Gas 5. Bring a pan of lightly salted water to the boil. Cut the parsnips, potatoes, carrots and sweet potatoes into chunks. Add them to the pan and bring the water back to the boil. Boil for 2 minutes, then drain the vegetables thoroughly.

2 Pour the olive oil into a large heavy roasting pan and place over a moderate heat. Add the vegetables, shallots and garlic. Fry, tossing the vegetables over the heat, until they are pale golden at the edges.

3 Add the mustard seeds, coriander seeds, cumin seeds and bay leaves. Cook for 1 minute, then season with salt and pepper. Transfer the roasting pan to the oven and roast for 45 minutes, turning occasionally, until the vegetables are crisp and golden and cooked through.

VARIATION

Vary the vegetables according to what is available. Try using swede (rutabaga) or pumpkin instead of, or as well as, the vegetables suggested.

Mexican Tortilla Parcels

Seeded green chillies add just a flicker of fire to the spicy filling in these parcels – perfect as an appetizer or snack.

<small>Serves 4</small>
675g/1½lb tomatoes
60ml/4 tbsp sunflower oil
1 large onion, thinly sliced
1 garlic clove, crushed
10ml/2 tsp cumin seeds
2 fresh green chillies, seeded
 and chopped
30ml/2 tbsp tomato purée (paste)
1 vegetable stock (bouillon) cube
200g/7oz can sweetcorn, drained
15ml/1 tbsp chopped fresh
 coriander (cilantro)
115g/4oz/1 cup grated
 Cheddar cheese
8 wheat tortillas
fresh coriander (cilantro) sprigs,
 shredded lettuce, fresh chillies
 and sour cream, to serve

1 Peel the tomatoes: place them in a heatproof bowl, add boiling water to cover and leave for 1 minute. Lift out with a slotted spoon and plunge into a bowl of cold water. Leave for 1 minute, then drain. Slip the skins off the tomatoes and chop the flesh.

2 Heat half the oil in a frying pan and fry the onion with the garlic and cumin seeds for 5 minutes, until the onion softens. Add the chillies and tomatoes, then stir in the tomato purée. Crumble the stock cube over, stir well and cook gently for 5 minutes, until the chilli is soft, but the tomato has not completely broken down. Stir in the sweetcorn and fresh coriander and heat gently to warm through. Keep warm.

3 Sprinkle grated cheese in the middle of each tortilla. Spoon some tomato mixture over the cheese. Fold over one edge of the tortilla then the sides and finally, the remaining edge to enclose the filling completely.

4 Heat the remaining oil in a separate frying pan and fry the tortillas for 1–2 minutes on each side until golden and crisp. Serve with coriander, lettuce, chillies and sour cream.

COOK'S TIP

Mexican wheat tortillas are available in most supermarkets. They are very useful to keep in the pantry as a wrapping for a variety of meat, chicken and vegetable mixtures.

Vegetable Couscous with Saffron and Harissa

A North African favourite, this spicy dish makes an excellent meal for vegetarians.

SERVES 4

45ml/3 tbsp olive oil
1 onion, chopped
2 garlic cloves, crushed
5ml/1 tsp ground cumin
5ml/1 tsp paprika
400g/14oz can chopped tomatoes
300ml/½ pint/1¼ cups
  vegetable stock
1 cinnamon stick
pinch of saffron threads
4 baby aubergines
  (eggplant), quartered
8 baby courgettes (zucchini), cut
  in half lengthwise
8 baby carrots
225g/8oz/1⅓ cups couscous
425g/15oz can chickpeas, drained
175g/6oz/¾ cup prunes
45ml/3 tbsp chopped parsley
45ml/3 tbsp chopped fresh
  coriander (cilantro)
10–15ml/2–3 tsp harissa
salt

1 Heat the olive oil in a large pan. Add the onions and garlic and cook gently for 5 minutes until soft. Add the cumin and paprika and cook, stirring, for 1 minute.

2 Add the tomatoes, stock, cinnamon stick, saffron, aubergines, courgettes and carrots. Season with salt. Bring to the boil, cover, lower the heat and cook for 20 minutes until the vegetables are just tender.

3 Line a steamer, metal sieve or colander with a double thickness of muslin (cheesecloth). Soak the couscous according to the instructions on the packet. Add the chickpeas and prunes to the vegetables and cook for 5 minutes. Fork the couscous to break up any lumps and spread it in the prepared steamer. Place on top of the vegetables, cover, and cook for 5 minutes until the couscous is hot.

4 Stir the parsley and coriander into the vegetables. Heap the couscous on to a warmed serving plate. Using a slotted spoon, arrange the vegetables on top. Spoon over a little sauce and toss gently to combine. Stir the harissa into the remaining sauce and serve separately.

Orange and Red Onion Salad with Cumin

Cumin and mint give this refreshing salad a Middle Eastern flavour. Choose small seedless oranges if you can.

<u>SERVES 6</u>

6 oranges
2 red onions
15ml/1 tbsp cumin seeds
5ml/1 tsp coarsely ground
  black pepper
15ml/1 tbsp chopped fresh mint
90ml/6 tbsp olive oil
salt
fresh mint sprigs, to serve
black olives, to serve

1 Slice the oranges thinly, working over a bowl to catch any juice. Then, holding each orange slice in turn over the bowl, cut round with scissors to remove the peel and pith. Slice the onions thinly and separate the rings.

COOK'S TIP

It is important to let the salad stand for 2 hours, so that the flavours develop and the onion softens slightly. However, do not leave the salad for much longer than this before serving.

2 Arrange the orange and onion slices in layers in a shallow dish, sprinkling each layer with cumin seeds, black pepper, mint, olive oil and salt to taste. Pour over the orange juice left over from slicing the oranges.

3 Leave the salad to marinate in a cool place for about 2 hours. Just before serving, sprinkle the salad with the mint sprigs and black olives.

Spanish Salad with Capers and Olives

Make this refreshing salad in the summer when tomatoes are sweet and full of flavour.

<u>SERVES 4</u>

4 tomatoes
¹/₂ cucumber
1 bunch spring onions (scallions)
1 bunch purslane or
  watercress, washed
8 pimiento-stuffed olives
30ml/2 tbsp drained capers
DRESSING
30ml/2 tbsp red wine vinegar
5ml/1 tsp paprika
2.5ml/¹/₂ tsp ground cumin
1 garlic clove, crushed
75ml/5 tbsp olive oil
salt and ground black pepper

1 Peel the tomatoes: place them in a heatproof bowl, add boiling water to cover and leave for 1 minute. Lift out with a slotted spoon and immediately plunge into a bowl of cold water. Leave for 1 minute, then drain. Slip the skins off the tomatoes, discard the seeds and dice the flesh finely. Put in a salad bowl.

2 Peel the cucumber, dice it finely and then add it to the tomatoes. Trim and chop half of the spring onions, add them to the salad bowl and mix together lightly.

3 Break the purslane or watercress into small sprigs. Add to the tomato mixture, with the olives and capers. Make the dressing. Mix the wine vinegar, paprika, cumin and garlic in a bowl. Whisk in the oil and add salt and pepper to taste. Pour over the salad and toss lightly. Serve the salad with the remaining spring onions.

COOK'S TIP

Serve this salad as soon as possible after adding the dressing.

Gado Gado

The peanut sauce on this traditional Indonesian salad owes its flavour to galangal, an aromatic rhizome that resembles ginger.

SERVES 4

250g/9oz white cabbage, shredded
4 carrots, cut into thin batons
4 celery sticks, cut into
  thin batons
250g/9oz/4 cups beansprouts
½ cucumber, cut into thin batons
fried onion, salted peanuts and
  sliced chilli, to garnish
PEANUT SAUCE
15ml/1 tbsp oil
1 small onion, finely chopped
1 garlic clove, crushed
1 small piece galangal, peeled
  and grated
5ml/1 tsp ground cumin
1.5ml/¼ tsp chilli powder
5ml/1 tsp tamarind paste
  or lime juice
60ml/4 tbsp crunchy
  peanut butter
5ml/1 tsp light brown sugar

1 Steam the cabbage, carrots and celery for 3–4 minutes until just tender. Leave to cool. Spread out the beansprouts on a large serving dish. Arrange the cabbage, carrots, celery and cucumber on top.

2 Make the sauce. Heat the oil in a pan, add the onion and garlic and cook gently for 5 minutes until soft. Stir in the galangal, cumin and chilli powder and cook for 1 minute more. Add the tamarind paste or lime juice, peanut butter and sugar. Mix well.

COOK'S TIPS

As long as the sauce remains the same, the vegetables can be altered at the whim of the cook and to reflect the contents of the vegetable rack or chiller. Pour the sauce over the salad and toss lightly or serve it in a separate bowl.

3 Heat gently, stirring occasionally and adding a little hot water, if necessary, to make a coating sauce. Spoon a little of the sauce over the vegetables and garnish with fried onions, peanuts and sliced chilli. Serve the rest of the sauce separately.

Sesame Duck and Noodle Salad

This salad is complete in itself and makes a lovely summer lunch. The marinade is a marvellous blend of spices.

SERVES 4

2 duck breast portions
15ml/1 tbsp oil
150g/5oz sugar snap peas
2 carrots, cut into
  7.5cm/3in sticks
225g/8oz medium egg noodles
6 spring onions (scallions), sliced
salt
30ml/2 tbsp fresh coriander
  (cilantro) sprigs, to garnish
MARINADE
15ml/1 tbsp sesame oil
5ml/1 tsp ground coriander
5ml/1 tsp five-spice powder
DRESSING
15ml/1 tbsp garlic vinegar
5ml/1 tsp light brown sugar
5ml/1 tsp soy sauce
15ml/1 tbsp toasted sesame
  seeds (see Cook's tip)
45ml/3 tbsp sunflower oil
30ml/2 tbsp sesame oil
ground black pepper

1 Slice the duck breast portions thinly and place them in a shallow dish. Mix all the ingredients for the marinade, pour over the duck and mix well to coat thoroughly. Cover and leave in a cool place for 30 minutes.

2 Heat the oil in a frying pan, add the slices of duck breast and stir-fry for 3–4 minutes until cooked. Set aside.

3 Bring a pan of lightly salted water to the boil. Place the sugar snap peas and carrots in a steamer that will fit on top of the pan. When the water boils, add the noodles. Place the steamer on top and steam the vegetables, while cooking the noodles for the time suggested on the packet. Set the steamed vegetables aside. Drain the noodles, refresh them under cold running water and drain again. Place them in a large serving bowl.

4 Make the dressing. Mix the vinegar, sugar, soy sauce and sesame seeds in a bowl. Add a generous grinding of black pepper, then whisk in the oils.

5 Pour the dressing over the noodles and mix well. Add the sugar snap peas, carrots, spring onions and duck slices and toss to mix. Sprinkle the coriander leaves over and serve.

COOK'S TIP

To toast the sesame seeds, place them in a dry heavy frying pan and heat gently, stirring frequently until they are lightly browned.

PIZZA, PASTA AND GRAINS

Chilli, Tomato and Olive Pasta

The sauce for this pasta packs a punch, thanks to the red chillies, anchovies and capers.

Serves 4

45ml/3 tbsp olive oil
2 garlic cloves, crushed
2 fresh red chillies, seeded
  and chopped
6 canned anchovy fillets, drained
675g/1½lb ripe tomatoes, peeled,
  seeded and chopped
30ml/2 tbsp sun-dried tomato
  purée (paste)
30ml/2 tbsp drained capers
115g/4oz/1 cup pitted black
  olives, coarsely chopped
350g/12oz/3 cups penne
salt and ground black pepper
chopped fresh basil, to garnish

1 Heat the oil in a pan and gently fry the garlic and chilli for 2–3 minutes. Add the anchovies, mashing them with a fork, then stir in the tomatoes, sun-dried tomato purée, capers and olives. Add salt and pepper to taste. Simmer gently, uncovered, for 20 minutes, stirring occasionally.

2 Meanwhile, bring a large pan of lightly salted water to the boil and cook the penne according to the instructions on the packet, or until *al dente*. Drain and immediately stir into the sauce. Mix thoroughly, tip into a heated serving dish, garnish with basil and serve immediately.

> #### COOK'S TIP
> *If ripe well-flavoured tomatoes are not available, use two 400g/14oz cans chopped tomatoes.*

Spaghettini with Garlic and Olive Oil

It is essential to use a good quality virgin olive oil and a brightly coloured fresh red chilli for this simply delicious pasta sauce.

Serves 4

350g/12oz spaghettini
75ml/5 tbsp virgin olive oil
3 garlic cloves, finely chopped
1 fresh red chilli, seeded
  and chopped
75g/3oz/1½ cups drained sun-
  dried tomatoes in oil, chopped
30ml/2 tbsp chopped fresh
  flat leaf parsley
salt and ground black pepper
freshly grated Parmesan cheese,
  to serve

1 Bring a large pan of lightly salted water to the boil. Add the pasta and cook according to the instructions on the packet, or until *al dente*. Towards the end of the cooking time, heat the oil in a second large pan. Add the garlic and chilli and cook gently for 2–3 minutes. Stir in the sun-dried tomatoes and remove from the heat.

> #### COOK'S TIP
> *Save the oil from the jar of sun-dried tomatoes for adding to salad dressings.*

2 Drain the pasta thoroughly and add to the hot oil. Return to the heat and cook for 2–3 minutes, tossing the pasta to coat the strands in the sauce. Season with salt and pepper, stir in the parsley and transfer to a warmed serving bowl. Sprinkle with grated Parmesan cheese and serve.

Pastitsio

Macaroni in a cheese sauce is layered with cinnamon and cumin-spiced beef to make a Greek version of lasagne.

SERVES 4–6

225g/8oz/2 cups macaroni
30ml/2 tbsp olive oil
1 large onion, finely chopped
2 garlic cloves, crushed
450g/1lb minced (ground) steak
300ml/½ pint/1¼ cups beef stock
10ml/2 tsp tomato purée (paste)
5ml/1 tsp ground cinnamon
5ml/1 tsp ground cumin
15ml/1 tbsp chopped fresh mint
50g/2oz/¼ cup butter
40g/1½oz/⅓ cup plain (all-
 purpose) flour
120ml/4fl oz/½ cup milk
120ml/4fl oz/½ cup natural (plain)
 yogurt
175g/6oz/1½ cups grated
 Kefalotiri cheese
salt and ground black pepper

1 Bring a pan of salted water to the boil. Cook the macaroni for 8 minutes, or until *al dente*. Drain and rinse under cold water. Preheat the oven to 190°C/375°F/Gas 5.

2 Heat the oil in a frying pan, add the onion and garlic and cook for 8–10 minutes until soft. Add the steak and stir until browned. Stir in the stock, tomato purée, cinnamon, cumin and mint, with salt and pepper to taste. Cook gently for 10–15 minutes until the sauce is thick and flavoursome.

3 Melt the butter in a pan. Stir in the flour and cook for 1 minute. Remove the pan from the heat and gradually stir in the milk and yogurt. Return the pan to the heat and cook gently for 5 minutes. Stir in half the cheese and season with salt and pepper. Stir the macaroni into the cheese sauce.

COOK'S TIP

If Kefalotiri cheese is unavailable, use a well-flavoured Cheddar cheese or similar.

4 Spread half the macaroni mixture over the base of a large gratin dish. Cover with the meat sauce and top with the remaining macaroni. Sprinkle the remaining cheese over the top and bake for 45 minutes or until golden brown on top.

Hot Pepperoni Pizza

There is nothing more mouth-watering than a freshly baked pizza, especially when the topping includes pepperoni and red chillies.

SERVES 4

225g/8oz/2 cups strong white (bread) flour
10ml/2 tsp easy-blend (rapid-rise) dried yeast
5ml/1 tsp sugar
2.5ml/$^{1}/_{2}$ tsp salt
15ml/1 tbsp olive oil
175ml/6fl oz/$^{3}/_{4}$ cup mixed lukewarm milk and water

TOPPING

400g/14oz can chopped tomatoes
2 garlic cloves, crushed
5ml/1 tsp dried oregano
225g/8oz/2 cups coarsely grated mozzarella cheese
2 dried red chillies, crumbled
225g/8oz pepperoni, sliced
30ml/2 tbsp drained capers
fresh oregano, to garnish

1 Sift the flour into a bowl. Stir in the yeast, sugar and salt. Make a well in the centre. Stir the olive oil into the milk and water, then stir the mixture into the flour. Mix to a soft dough.

2 Knead the dough on a lightly floured surface for 5–10 minutes until it is smooth and elastic. Return it to the clean, lightly oiled, bowl and cover with clear film (plastic wrap). Leave in a warm place for about 30 minutes or until the dough has doubled in bulk.

3 Preheat the oven to 220°C/425°F/ Gas 7. Turn the dough out on to a lightly floured surface and knead lightly for 1 minute. Divide it in half and roll each piece out to a 25cm/ 10in circle. Place on lightly oiled pizza trays or baking sheets. To make the topping, mix the drained tomatoes, garlic and oregano in a bowl.

> COOK'S TIP
>
> *If time is short, use ready-made pizza bases or scone (US biscuit) bases.*

4 Spread half the mixture over each round, leaving a margin around the edge. Set half the mozzarella aside. Divide the rest between the pizzas. Bake for 7–10 minutes until the dough rim on each pizza is pale golden.

5 Sprinkle the crumbled chillies over the pizzas, then arrange the pepperoni slices and capers on top. Sprinkle with the remaining mozzarella. Return the pizzas to the oven and bake for 7–10 minutes more. Sprinkle over the oregano and serve at once.

Singapore Noodles

Dried mushrooms add an intense flavour to this lightly curried dish. Use Chinese mushrooms if possible.

SERVES 4

20g/¾oz/⅓ cup dried Chinese mushrooms
225g/8oz fine egg noodles
10ml/2 tsp sesame oil
45ml/3 tbsp groundnut (peanut) oil
2 garlic cloves, crushed
1 small onion, chopped
1 fresh green chilli, seeded and thinly sliced
10ml/2 tsp curry powder
115g/4oz green beans, trimmed and halved
115g/4oz/1 cup Chinese leaves (Chinese cabbage), shredded
4 spring onions (scallions), sliced
30ml/2 tbsp soy sauce
115g/4oz cooked prawns (shrimp), peeled
salt

1 Place the mushrooms in a bowl. Cover with warm water and soak for 30 minutes. Drain, reserving 30ml/2 tbsp of the soaking water, then slice.

2 Bring a pan of lightly salted water to the boil and cook the noodles according to the directions on the packet. Drain, tip into a bowl and toss with the sesame oil.

VARIATION

Ring the changes with the vegetables used in this dish. Try mangetouts (snow peas), broccoli, (bell) peppers or baby corn. The prawns can be omitted or substituted with ham.

3 Heat a wok and add the groundnut oil. When it is hot, stir-fry the garlic, onion and chilli for 3 minutes. Stir in the curry powder and cook for 1 minute. Add the mushrooms, green beans, Chinese leaves and spring onions. Stir-fry for 3–4 minutes until the vegetables are crisp-tender.

4 Add the noodles, soy sauce, reserved mushroom soaking water and prawns. Toss over the heat for about 2–3 minutes until the noodles and prawns are heated through.

Jambalaya

This popular Cajun dish has something in common with paella, but is distinguished by the addition of fiery spices.

SERVES 4

30ml/2 tbsp oil
225g/8oz skinless, boneless chicken, cubed
225g/8oz chorizo sausage, cut into chunks
3 celery sticks, chopped
1 red (bell) pepper, seeded and chopped
1 green (bell) pepper, seeded and chopped
1 quantity Cajun spice mix, including onion and garlic
250g/9oz/1¼ cups long grain rice
200g/7oz can chopped tomatoes
600ml/1 pint/2½ cups chicken stock
celery leaves, to garnish

1 Heat the oil in a large heavy frying pan. Add the chicken and chorizo sausage and fry until lightly browned. Remove from the pan with a slotted spoon and set aside. Add the celery and red and green peppers and fry for 2–3 minutes. Return the chicken and chorizo to the pan.

VARIATION

Raw tiger prawns (jumbo shrimp) can be added with the rice. Alternatively, duck and ham may be used instead of chicken and chorizo.

2 Stir in the Cajun spice mix and cook, stirring, for 2–3 minutes more. Stir in the rice and add the tomatoes and stock. Bring to the boil and stir.

3 Turn the heat to low, cover the pan and simmer gently for 15–20 minutes until the rice is tender and the liquid has been absorbed. Garnish and serve.

COOK'S TIP

This dish is very hot. If you like a milder result, use less Cajun spice mix.

Thai Fried Rice

This recipe uses jasmine rice which is sometimes known as Thai fragrant rice.

SERVES 4

50g/2oz/½ cup coconut
  milk powder
350g/12oz/1⅓ cups jasmine rice
30ml/2 tbsp groundnut (peanut) oil
2 garlic cloves, chopped
1 small onion, finely chopped
2.5cm/1in piece fresh root
  ginger, grated
225g/8oz skinless, boneless
  chicken breast portions, diced
1 red (bell) pepper, seeded
  and diced
115g/4oz/⅔ cup drained canned
  sweetcorn kernels
5ml/1 tsp chilli oil
15ml/1 tbsp hot curry powder
salt
2 eggs, beaten
spring onion (scallions), to garnish

1 In a pan, whisk the coconut milk powder into 475ml/16fl oz/2 cups water. Add the rice, bring to the boil and stir once. Lower the heat to a gentle simmer, cover and cook for 10 minutes or until the rice is tender and the liquid has been absorbed. Spread the rice on a baking sheet and leave until completely cold.

2 Heat the oil in a wok, add the garlic, onion and ginger and stir-fry for 2 minutes. Push the vegetables to the sides of the wok, add the chicken to the centre and stir-fry for 2 minutes. Add the rice and stir-fry over a high heat for 3 minutes more.

3 Stir in the pepper, sweetcorn, chilli oil, curry powder and season with salt. Toss over the heat for 1 minute. Stir in the beaten egg and cook for 1 minute more. Garnish with spring onion shreds and serve.

COOK'S TIPS

It is important that the rice is completely cold before it is fried and the oil should be very hot, or the rice will absorb too much oil. Add some sliced baby corn cobs along with the rice, if you like.

Pilau Rice with Whole Spices

This fragrant rice dish makes a perfect accompaniment to any Indian meal.

SERVES 4–6

generous pinch of saffron threads
600ml/1 pint/2½ cups hot
  chicken stock
50g/2oz/¼ cup butter
1 onion, chopped
1 garlic clove, crushed
½ cinnamon stick
6 cardamoms
1 bay leaf
250g/9oz/1¼ cups basmati rice,
  rinsed and drained
50g/2oz/⅓ cup sultanas
  (golden raisins)
15ml/1 tbsp oil
50g/2oz/½ cup cashew nuts

1 Add the saffron threads to the hot stock and set aside. Heat the butter in a large pan and fry the onion and garlic for 5 minutes. Stir in the cinnamon stick, cardamoms and bay leaf and cook for 2 minutes.

COOK'S TIP

To rinse the rice, stir it around in several changes of water until the water is clear. Drain thoroughly before cooking.

2 Add the rice and cook, stirring, for 2 minutes more. Pour in the stock and add the sultanas. Bring to the boil, stir, then lower the heat, cover and cook gently for 15 minutes or until the rice is tender and the liquid has all been absorbed.

3 Meanwhile, heat the oil in a frying pan and fry the cashew nuts until browned. Drain on kitchen paper. Sprinkle over the rice and serve.

Couscous Salad

This is a spicy variation on a classic tabbouleh, which is traditionally made with bulgur wheat, not couscous.

<u>SERVES 4</u>

45ml/3 tbsp olive oil
5 spring onions, chopped
1 garlic clove, crushed
5ml/1 tsp ground cumin
350ml/12fl oz/1½ cups
  vegetable stock
175g/6oz/1 cup couscous
2 tomatoes, peeled and chopped
60ml/4 tbsp chopped fresh parsley
60ml/4 tbsp chopped fresh mint
1 fresh green chilli, seeded and
  finely chopped
30ml/2 tbsp lemon juice
salt and ground black pepper
toasted pine nuts and grated
  lemon rind, to garnish
crisp lettuce leaves, to serve

1 Heat the oil in a pan. Add the spring onions and crushed garlic. Stir in the cumin and cook for 1 minute. Add the stock and bring to the boil.

2 Remove the pan from the heat, stir in the couscous, cover the pan and leave it to stand for 10 minutes, until the couscous has swelled and all the liquid has been absorbed. If using instant couscous, follow the instructions on the packet.

3 Tip the couscous into a bowl. Stir in the tomatoes, parsley, mint, chilli and lemon juice, with salt and pepper to taste. If possible, leave to stand for up to an hour to allow the flavours to develop fully.

4 To serve, line a bowl with lettuce leaves and spoon the couscous salad into the centre. Sprinkle with the toasted pine nuts and grated lemon rind, to garnish.

Bulgur Wheat and Lentil Pilaff

Bulgur wheat is a very useful pantry ingredient. It has a nutty taste and texture and only needs soaking before serving in a salad or warming through for a hot dish.

SERVES 4

115g/4oz/½ cup green lentils
115g/4oz/⅔ cup bulgur wheat
5ml/1 tsp ground coriander
5ml/1 tsp ground cinnamon
1 tbsp olive oil
225g/8oz rindless streaky (fatty)
  bacon rashers (strips), chopped
1 red onion, chopped
1 garlic clove, crushed
5ml/1 tsp cumin seeds
30ml/2 tbsp coarsely chopped
  fresh parsley
salt and ground black pepper

COOK'S TIP

Look for Puy lentils, which have a superior flavour, aroma and texture.

1 Soak the lentils and bulgur wheat separately in cold water for 1 hour, then drain. Tip the lentils into a pan. Stir in the coriander, cinnamon and 475ml/16fl oz/2 cups water. Bring to the boil, then simmer until the lentils are tender and the liquid has been absorbed.

2 Meanwhile, heat the olive oil and fry the bacon until crisp. Remove and drain on kitchen paper. Add the red onion and garlic to the oil remaining in the pan and fry for 10 minutes until soft and golden brown. Stir in the cumin seeds and cook for 1 minute more. Return the bacon to the pan.

3 Stir the drained bulgur wheat into the cooked lentils, then add the mixture to the frying pan. Season with salt and pepper and heat through. Stir in the parsley and serve.

BREADS, BUNS AND TEABREADS

Focaccia with Green Peppercorns and Rock Salt

The combination of green peppercorns and a fruity olive oil gives these open-textured Italian flatbreads a delectable flavour.

MAKES 1 LOAF

350g/12oz/3 cups strong white (bread) flour
2.5ml/½ tsp salt
10ml/2 tsp easy-blend (rapid-rise) dried yeast
10ml/2 tsp drained green peppercorns in brine, lightly crushed
25ml/1½ tbsp fruity extra virgin olive oil
about 250ml/8fl oz/1 cup lukewarm water
20ml/4 tsp roughly crushed rock salt, for the topping
basil leaves, to garnish

1 Sift the flour and salt into a mixing bowl. Stir in the yeast and crushed peppercorns. Make a well in the centre and stir in 15ml/1 tbsp of the olive oil, with enough of the lukewarm water to make a soft dough.

2 Turn the dough out on to a lightly floured surface and knead for about 10 minutes until smooth and elastic. Return to the clean, oiled bowl, cover with clear film (plastic wrap) and leave in a warm place until doubled in bulk.

3 Turn the dough out on to a floured surface and knead lightly for 2–3 minutes. Place on an oiled baking sheet and pat out to a rough oval. Cover with a clean cloth and leave for 30 minutes until the dough puffs up.

4 Preheat the oven to 190°C/375°F/ Gas 5. With your fingers, make a few dimples in the surface of the dough. Drizzle the remaining olive oil over, then sprinkle with the crushed rock salt. Bake the focaccia for 25–30 minutes until pale gold. Sprinkle the loaf with basil leaves and serve warm.

COOK'S TIP

Instead of one large loaf, you could make two medium or four individual loaves.

Spiced Naan Bread

Indian naan bread is traditionally baked in a fiercely hot oven called a tandoor. However, good results can be achieved using a combination of a hot oven and a grill.

MAKES 6

450g/1lb/4 cups plain (**all-purpose**) flour
5ml/1 tsp baking powder
2.5ml/½ tsp salt
1 sachet easy-blend (**rapid-rise**) dried yeast
5ml/1 tsp caster (**superfine**) sugar
5ml/1 tsp fennel seeds
10ml/2 tsp black onion seeds
5ml/1 tsp cumin seeds
150ml/¼ pint/⅔ cup lukewarm milk
30ml/2 tbsp oil, plus extra for brushing
150ml/¼ pint/⅔ cup natural (**plain**) yogurt
1 egg, beaten

VARIATION
Vary the spices used by adding chopped chilli to the mixture, or sprinkling with poppy seeds before baking.

1 Sift the flour, baking powder and salt into a mixing bowl. Stir in the yeast, sugar, fennel seeds, black onion seeds and cumin seeds. Make a well in the centre. Stir the lukewarm milk into the flour mixture, then add the oil, yogurt and beaten egg. Mix to form a ball of dough.

2 Turn the dough out on to a lightly floured surface and knead it for 10 minutes until smooth. Return to the clean, lightly oiled bowl and roll to coat with oil. Cover the bowl with clear film (plastic wrap) and set aside until the dough has doubled in size.

3 Put a heavy baking sheet in the oven and preheat the oven to 240°C/475°F/Gas 9. Also preheat the grill (broiler). Knead the dough again lightly and divide it into 6 pieces. Keep 5 pieces covered while working with the sixth. Quickly roll the piece of dough out to a tear-drop shape (see right), brush lightly with oil and slap the naan on to the hot baking sheet. Repeat with the remaining dough.

4 Bake the naan in the oven for 3 minutes until puffed up, then place the baking sheet under the grill for about 30 seconds or until the naan are lightly browned. Serve hot or warm as a side dish to an Indian curry.

Chilli Cheese Muffins

These muffins are flavoured with chilli purée, which is available in tubes or jars.

MAKES 12

115g/4oz/1 cup self-raising (self-rising) flour
15ml/1 tbsp baking powder
5ml/1 tsp salt
225g/8oz/2 cups fine corn meal
150g/5oz/1¼ cups grated mature (sharp) Cheddar cheese
50g/2oz/4 tbsp butter, melted
2 large (US extra large) eggs, beaten
5ml/1 tsp chilli purée (paste)
1 garlic clove, crushed
300ml/½ pint/1¼ cups milk

1 Preheat the oven to 200°C/400°F/Gas 6. Thoroughly grease 12 deep muffin tins (pans) or line the tins with paper cake cases. Sift the flour, baking powder and salt into a bowl, then stir in the corn meal and 115g/4oz/1 cup of the grated cheese.

2 Pour the melted butter into a bowl and stir in the eggs, chilli purée, crushed garlic and milk.

3 Pour on to the dry ingredients and mix quickly until just combined.

4 Spoon the batter into the prepared muffin tins, sprinkle the remaining cheese on top and bake for 20 minutes until risen and golden brown. Leave to cool for a few minutes before turning the muffins out on to a wire rack to cool completely.

COOK'S TIP

Take care not to over-mix the muffin mixture or the muffins will be heavy. Stir the mixture just enough to combine the ingredients roughly.

Chilli Cornbread

This golden yellow cornbread spiked with chilli makes an excellent accompaniment to soups and salads.

MAKES 9 SLICES

2 eggs
450ml/¾ pint/1⅞ cups buttermilk
50g/2oz/¼ cup butter, melted
65g/2½oz/½ cup plain (all-purpose) flour
2.5ml/½ tsp ground mace
5ml/1 tsp bicarbonate of soda (baking soda)
10ml/2 tsp salt
250g/9oz/2¼ cups fine corn meal
2 fresh red chillies, seeded and finely chopped
shredded red chillies and sea salt, to garnish

1 Preheat the oven to 200°C/400°F/Gas 6. Line and grease a 23 x 7.5cm/9 x 3in loaf tin (pan). In a large bowl, whisk the eggs until frothy, then whisk in the buttermilk and melted butter.

2 Sift the flour, mace, bicarbonate of soda and salt together and gradually stir into the egg mixture. Fold in the corn meal a little at a time, then stir in the fresh chillies.

3 Pour the mixture into the prepared tin and bake for 25–30 minutes until the top is firm to the touch.

4 Leave the loaf to cool in the tin for a few minutes before turning out. Sprinkle over the chillies and sea salt, then cut into slices and serve warm.

COOK'S TIP

For a loaf with a more rustic appearance, use medium or coarse corn meal.

Chelsea Buns

These traditional sticky buns, packed with spice and fruit, are always popular.

MAKES 9

225g/8oz/2 cups strong white (bread) flour
10ml/2 tsp easy-blend (rapid-rise) dried yeast
5ml/1 tsp caster (superfine) sugar
2.5ml/½ tsp salt
25g/1oz/2 tbsp unsalted (sweet) butter, softened
120ml4fl oz/½ cup lukewarm milk
1 egg, beaten
75g/3oz/¾ cup icing (confectioners') sugar

> COOK'S TIP
>
> *Don't be tempted to try to hurry the rising process by putting the dough in an oven or other hot place to rise. Excessive heat will kill the yeast.*

FILLING

50g/2oz/¼ cup unsalted (sweet) butter, softened
50g/2oz/¼ cup light brown sugar
115g/4oz/⅔ cup mixed dried fruit
5ml/1 tsp ground cinnamon
2.5ml/½ tsp ground nutmeg
1.25ml/¼ tsp ground cloves

1 Grease an 18cm/7in square cake tin (pan). Sift the flour into a mixing bowl. Stir in the yeast, sugar and salt. Rub in the butter until the mixture resembles breadcrumbs, then make a well in the centre and pour in the warm milk and beaten egg. Beat together vigorously to make a soft dough.

2 Knead the dough on a floured surface for 5–10 minutes until smooth. Return it to the clean, lightly oiled bowl, cover with clear film (plastic wrap) and leave in a warm place until doubled in size. Turn out on to a floured surface. Knead lightly and roll out to give a rectangle. This should measure about 30 x 23cm/12 x 9in.

3 Spread the dough with the softened butter and sprinkle with the brown sugar, dried fruit, cinnamon, nutmeg and ground cloves. Roll up from a long side and cut into 9 pieces. Place in the prepared tin, cut sides up. Cover with lightly oiled clear film and leave in a warm place for 45 minutes or until the buns are well risen.

4 Preheat the oven to 190°C/375°F/ Gas 5. Bake the buns for 30 minutes until golden. Leave to cool in the tin for 10 minutes, then transfer, in one piece, to a wire rack to cool. Mix the icing sugar with enough water to make a thin glaze and brush over the buns. Pull the buns apart to serve.

Cornish Saffron Buns

Saffron gives these buns a brilliant golden colour and a distinctive flavour.

MAKES 12

175ml/6fl oz/¾ cup milk
2.5ml/½ tsp saffron threads
60ml/4 tbsp caster (superfine) sugar
400g/14oz/3½ cups strong white (bread) flour
1 sachet easy-blend (rapid-rise) dried yeast
2.5ml/½ tsp salt
40g/1½oz/3 tbsp butter, melted
2 eggs, beaten

1 Put the milk and saffron threads in a pan and gradually bring to the boil. Remove from the heat, stir in the sugar and leave for about 5 minutes until the mixture is lukewarm.

2 Sift the flour into a bowl and stir in the yeast and salt. Make a well in the centre. Add the melted butter and half the egg to the milk, then mix with the dry ingredients to make a dough. Turn the dough out on to a lightly floured surface and knead for 10 minutes.

> COOK'S TIP
>
> *Buy fresh saffron for the best flavour and do not keep it for too long.*

3 Divide the dough into 12 pieces and roll into balls. Place on greased baking sheets and cover with a cloth. Leave to rise until the buns have doubled in size.

4 Preheat the oven to 190°C/375°F/ Gas 5. Glaze the tops of the buns with the remaining beaten egg and bake for 15–20 minutes until they are golden and sound hollow when rapped with your knuckle underneath. Cool on a wire rack.

Stollen

Stollen is an Austrian spiced fruit bread with a marzipan filling. Although it is traditionally served at Christmas, it is delicious at any time, served warm or cold or toasted and buttered.

SERVES 10

40g/1½oz/¼ cup glacé (candied)
  cherries, rinsed and dried
50g/2oz/¼ cup currants
75g/3oz/½ cup raisins
40g/1½oz/¼ cup chopped
  mixed (candied) peel
30ml/2 tbsp rum
50g/2oz/¼ cup butter
175ml/6fl oz/¾ cup milk
30ml/2 tbsp caster (superfine) sugar
375g/12oz/3 cups strong white
  (bread) flour
1.5ml/¼ tsp salt
2.5ml/½ tsp ground nutmeg
2.5ml/½ tsp ground cinnamon
seeds from 3 cardamoms, crushed
1 sachet easy-blend (rapid-rise)
  dried yeast
grated rind of 1 lemon
1 egg, beaten
40g/1½oz/⅓ cup flaked
  (sliced) almonds
175g/6oz marzipan
melted butter, for brushing
sifted icing (confectioners') sugar

1 Quarter the cherries. Place them with the currants, raisins and peel in a bowl. Stir in the rum. Mix the butter, milk and caster sugar in a pan and heat until the sugar has dissolved and the butter has melted. Cool until lukewarm.

2 Sift the flour, salt, nutmeg and cinnamon into a bowl. Add the cardamom seeds. Stir in the yeast. Make a well in the centre and stir in the milk mixture, lemon rind and beaten egg. Beat to form a soft dough.

3 Turn on to a floured surface. With floured hands, knead the dough for about 5 minutes. It will be quite sticky, so add more flour if necessary. Knead the soaked fruit and flaked almonds into the dough until just combined.

4 Return the dough to the clean, lightly oiled bowl, cover with clear film (plastic wrap) and leave in a warm place for up to 3 hours until it has doubled in size.

5 Turn the dough on to a lightly floured surface. Knead for about 1–2 minutes, then roll out to a 25cm/10in square. Roll the marzipan to a sausage shape slightly shorter than the length of the dough and place in the centre. Fold one side over to cover the marzipan and repeat with the other side, overlapping in the centre. Seal the ends.

6 Place the roll, seam-side down, on a greased baking sheet. Cover with oiled clear film and leave in a warm place until doubled in size. Preheat the oven to 190°C/375°F/Gas 5.

7 Bake the stollen for 40 minutes, or until it is golden and sounds hollow when rapped underneath. Brush the hot stollen generously with melted butter and dredge heavily with sifted icing sugar.

Orange and Coriander Brioches

The warm spicy flavour of coriander combines particularly well with orange.

MAKES 12

225g/8oz/2 cups strong white (bread) flour
10ml/2 tsp easy-blend (rapid-rise) dried yeast
2.5ml/$\frac{1}{2}$ tsp salt
15ml/1 tbsp caster (superfine) sugar
10ml/2 tsp coriander seeds, coarsely ground
grated rind of 1 orange
2 eggs, beaten
50g/2oz/$\frac{1}{4}$ cup unsalted (sweet) butter, melted
1 small egg, beaten, to glaze

1 Grease 12 individual brioche tins (pans). Sift the flour into a bowl and stir in the yeast, salt, sugar, coriander and orange rind. Make a well in the centre, pour in 30ml/2 tbsp lukewarm water, the eggs and butter and beat to make a soft dough. Turn the dough on to a floured surface and knead for 5 minutes until smooth and elastic. Return to the clean, oiled bowl, cover with clear film (plastic wrap) and leave in a warm place for 1 hour until doubled in size.

2 Turn on to a floured surface, knead again briefly and roll into a sausage. Cut into 12 pieces. Break off one-quarter of each piece and set aside. Shape the larger pieces of dough into balls and place in the prepared tins.

3 With a floured wooden spoon, press a hole in each dough ball. Shape each small piece of dough into a little plug and press into the holes.

COOK'S TIP

These individual brioches look particularly attractive if they are made in special brioche tins (pans). However, they can also be made in bun tins or muffin tins.

4 Place the brioche tins on a baking sheet. Cover with lightly oiled clear film and leave in a warm place until the dough rises almost to the top of the tins. Preheat the oven to 220°C/425°F/ Gas 7. Brush the brioches with beaten egg and bake for 15 minutes until golden brown. Sprinkle over extra shreds of orange rind to decorate, if you like, and serve the brioches warm with butter.

CAKES

Spiced Caribbean Christmas Cake

There's a taste of the tropics in this spicy fruit cake spiked with brandy, rum and port.

MAKES 1 X 23CM/9IN CAKE

675g/1½ lb luxury dried
  mixed fruit
115g/4oz/⅔ cup ready-to-eat
  prunes, chopped
115g/4oz/⅔ cup ready-to-eat
  dried mango or papaya
  pieces, chopped
50g/2oz/½ cup glacé (candied)
  cherries, quartered
45ml/3 tbsp brandy
45ml/3 tbsp rum
45ml/3 tbsp port
60ml/4 tbsp cherry brandy
15ml/1 tbsp mixed (apple
  pie) spice
2.5ml/½ tsp salt
10ml/2 tsp vanilla essence (extract)
15ml/1 tbsp treacle (molasses)
250g/9oz/2¼ cups self-raising
  (self-rising) flour
250g/9oz/1½ cups demerara
  (raw) sugar
250g/9oz/generous 1 cup
  butter, softened
6 eggs, beaten

1 Combine the mixed fruit, prunes, mango or papaya pieces and glacé cherries in a pan. Add the brandy, rum, port, cherry brandy, mixed spice, salt, vanilla essence, treacle and 60ml/4 tbsp water. Bring to the boil, then simmer gently for 15 minutes.

2 Set the fruit mixture aside to cool. Leave overnight or, if time allows, place in a large screw-top jar and chill for up to 1 week.

3 Preheat the oven to 140°C/275°F/Gas 1. Grease and line a 23cm/9in round cake tin (pan). Sift the flour into a large mixing bowl. Add the demerara sugar, softened butter and eggs. Beat the mixture thoroughly until well combined. Gradually fold in the macerated fruit mixture.

COOK'S TIP

This is a very rich moist cake and does not need marzipan or icing (frosting), but, if you want to decorate it, a glazed nut and glacé (candied) fruit topping looks and tastes good.

4 Pour the mixture into the prepared tin, level the surface and bake for 3½–4 hours until cooked through. Place a sheet of greaseproof (waxed) paper over the cake after about 3 hours if it is browning too quickly.

5 Leave the cake to cool in the tin for 45 minutes, then transfer it to a wire rack to cool completely. Wrap in greaseproof paper and store in an air-tight container. If possible, keep the cake for 1 month before cutting.

Honey Spice Cake

Use a strongly flavoured honey, such as chestnut honey, which will not be over- whelmed by the spices.

MAKES 8–10 SLICES

150g/5oz/²⁄₃ cup butter
115g/4oz/¹⁄₂ cup light
  brown sugar
175g/6oz/³⁄₄ cup clear honey
200g/7oz/1³⁄₄ cups self-raising
  (self-rising) flour
2.5ml/¹⁄₂ tsp ground ginger
2.5ml/¹⁄₂ tsp ground cinnamon
1.5ml/¹⁄₄ tsp caraway seeds
1.5ml/¹⁄₄ tsp ground cloves
2 eggs, beaten
350g/12oz/3 cups icing
  (confectioners') sugar
crushed sugar, to decorate

COOK'S TIP

This cake benefits from being kept for a day before eating.

1 Preheat the oven to 180°C/350°F/ Gas 4. Grease a 900ml/1¹⁄₂ pint/ 3³⁄₄ cup fluted mould. Put the butter, sugar, honey and 15ml/1 tbsp water into a pan. Heat gently until the butter has melted and the sugar has dissolved. Remove from the heat and cool for 10 minutes.

2 Sift the flour into a bowl and mix in the ginger, cinnamon, caraway seeds and ground cloves. Make a well in the centre. Pour in the honey mixture and the eggs and beat well until smooth. Pour the batter into the mould.

3 Bake for 40–50 minutes until the cake is well risen and a skewer inserted into the centre comes out clean. Leave to cool in the mould for 2–3 minutes, then remove to a wire rack to cool.

4 Make the icing (frosting). Sift the icing sugar into a bowl. Stir in enough warm water to make a smooth icing. Spoon carefully over the cake so that it is evenly coated. Decorate with sugar.

Lemon Poppy Seed Cake

Pouring lemon syrup over this makes it marvellously moist, while the poppy seeds add texture and extra flavour.

MAKES 12 SQUARES OR DIAMONDS

40g/1½oz/⅓ cup poppy seeds
115g/4oz/½ cup butter, softened
175g/6oz/¾ cup caster
 (superfine) sugar
2 eggs, beaten
finely grated rind of 1 lemon
175g/6oz/1½ cups self-raising
 (self-rising) flour, sifted
60ml/4 tbsp milk
TOPPING
juice of 1 lemon
115g/4oz/½ cup granulated sugar
lemon rind, to decorate

1 Preheat the oven to 180°C/350°F/ Gas 4. Grease a 23 x 18cm/9 x 7in cake tin (pan), about 2.5cm/1in deep. Line it with baking parchment. Grind the seeds in a coffee grinder or place between 2 sheets of clear film (plastic wrap) and crush with a rolling pin.

2 Beat the butter and sugar in a bowl until light and fluffy. Gradually beat in the eggs. Stir in the lemon rind. Fold in the flour, alternately with the milk, then fold in the poppy seeds.

3 Spoon the mixture into the prepared tin and level the surface. Bake for about 45 minutes until the cake is well risen and pale golden.

COOK'S TIP

If you warm the lemon in a microwave for a few seconds on High, it will yield more juice.

4 While the cake is baking, mix the lemon juice and sugar in a bowl. Remove the cake from the oven and, without taking it out of the tin, immediately pour the lemon mixture evenly over the surface.

5 Leave the cake in the tin until completely cold, then cut into squares or diamonds. Decorate with fine strips of lemon rind.

Ginger Cake

Three forms of ginger make this the ultimate spice cake.

MAKES 12 SQUARES

225g/8oz/2 cups self-raising (self-rising) flour
15ml/1 tbsp ground ginger
5ml/1 tsp ground cinnamon
2.5ml/½ tsp bicarbonate of soda (baking soda)
115g/4oz/½ cup butter
115g/4oz/½ cup light brown sugar
2 eggs
25ml/1½ tbsp golden (light corn) syrup
25ml/1½ tbsp milk
TOPPING
6 pieces stem (crystallized) ginger, plus 20ml/4 tsp syrup, from the jar
115g/4oz/1 cup icing (confectioners') sugar
lemon juice

1   Preheat the oven to 160°C/325°F/ Gas 3. Grease and line an 18cm/7in square cake tin (pan).

2   Sift the flour, ginger, cinnamon and bicarbonate of soda into a bowl. Rub in the butter, then stir in the sugar.

3   Make a well in the centre. In a bowl, whisk together the eggs, syrup and milk. Pour into the dry ingredients, then beat until smooth and glossy.

4   Spoon into the prepared tin and bake for 45–50 minutes until well risen and firm to the touch. Leave in the tin for 30 minutes, then remove to a wire rack to cool completely.

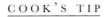

COOK'S TIP

This cake benefits from being kept in an airtight container for a day before eating.

5   Cut each piece of stem ginger into quarters and arrange the pieces on top of the cake.

6   Sift the icing sugar into a bowl and stir in the ginger syrup and enough lemon juice to make a smooth icing (frosting). Put the icing into a greaseproof (waxed) paper piping (icing) bag and drizzle over the top of the cake. Leave to set, then cut the cake into squares.

Ginger-topped Shortbread Fingers

Topping a ginger shortbread base with a sticky ginger topping may be gilding the lily, but it tastes delicious!

MAKES ABOUT 40

225g/8oz/2 cups plain
  (all-purpose) flour
5ml/1 tsp ground ginger
90ml/6 tbsp caster (superfine) sugar
3 pieces stem (crystallized)
  ginger, finely chopped
175g/6oz/³⁄₄ cup butter
15ml/1 tbsp golden (light
  corn) syrup
50g/2oz/¹⁄₄ cup butter
60ml/4 tbsp icing (confectioners')
  sugar, sifted
5ml/1 tsp ground ginger

1 Preheat the oven to 180°C/350°F/Gas 4. Grease a shallow 28 x 18cm/11 x 7in baking tin (pan). Sift the flour and ground ginger into a bowl and stir in the sugar and stem ginger.

2 Rub in the butter until the mixture begins to stick together. Press the mixture into the prepared tin and smooth over the top with a palette knife (metal spatula). Bake for about 40 minutes until the ginger shortbread base is very lightly browned.

3 Make the topping. Put the syrup and butter in a small pan. Heat gently until both have melted. Stir in the icing sugar and ginger. Remove the cake tin from the oven and pour the topping over the base while both are still hot. Allow to cool slightly, then cut into fingers. Transfer to wire racks to cool completely.

COOK'S TIP

You can use the syrup from the jar of stem ginger instead of golden syrup.

Apple and Cinnamon Muffins

These spicy muffins are quick and easy to make and are perfect for serving for breakfast or tea.

MAKES 6 LARGE MUFFINS

1 egg, beaten
45ml/3 tbsp caster (superfine) sugar
120ml/4fl oz/¹⁄₂ cup milk
50g/2oz/¹⁄₄ cup butter, melted
150g/5oz/1¹⁄₄ cups plain
  (all-purpose) flour
7.5ml/1¹⁄₂ tsp baking powder
1.5ml/¹⁄₄ tsp salt
2.5ml/¹⁄₂ tsp ground cinnamon
2 small eating apples, peeled,
  cored and finely chopped
TOPPING
12 brown sugar cubes, crushed
5ml/1 tsp ground cinnamon

1 Preheat the oven to 200°C/400°F/Gas 6. Line 6 large muffin tins with paper cases. Mix the egg, sugar, milk and melted butter in a large bowl. Sift in the flour, baking powder, salt and cinnamon. Add the chopped apple and mix roughly.

2 Spoon the muffin mixture into the prepared muffin cases. Make the topping by mixing the crushed sugar cubes with the cinnamon. Sprinkle over the uncooked muffins. Bake for 30–35 minutes until well risen and golden. Cool on a wire rack.

COOK'S TIP

Do not overmix the muffin mixture – it should be lumpy.

Vanilla Streusel Bars

The crumbly topping on this cake makes a crunchy contrast to the moist vanilla-flavoured sponge lying underneath.

MAKES ABOUT 25

175g/6oz/1½ cups self-raising (self-rising) flour
5ml/1 tsp baking powder
175g/6oz/¾ cup butter, softened
175g/6oz/¾ cup vanilla sugar
3 eggs, beaten
7.5ml/1½ tsp vanilla essence (extract)
15–30ml/1–2 tbsp milk
STREUSEL TOPPING
115g/4oz/1 cup self-raising (self-rising) flour
75g/3oz/6 tbsp butter
75g/3oz/6 tbsp vanilla sugar
icing (confectioners') sugar, to finish

1 Preheat the oven to 180°C/350°F/ Gas 4. Grease and line a shallow 23 x 18cm/9 x 7in baking tin (pan).

2 Make the topping. Sift the flour into a bowl and rub in the butter until the mixture resembles coarse breadcrumbs. Stir in the vanilla sugar and set aside.

3 Sift the flour and baking powder into a bowl. Add the butter, vanilla sugar and eggs. Beat well until the mixture is smooth, adding the vanilla essence and just enough milk to give a soft dropping (pourable) consistency.

4 Spoon the mixture into the prepared tin. Sprinkle the streusel topping over the surface and press down to cover. Bake for 45–60 minutes until browned and firm. Cool in the tin for 5 minutes, then turn out on to a wire rack to cool completely. Cut into bars when cool.

COOK'S TIP

Cover the cake loosely with foil if the topping browns too quickly.

Chocolate Lebkuchen

*Cut this nutty cake into small squares
to serve with after-dinner coffee.*

MAKES 24

3 eggs

200g/7oz/1 cup caster
  (superfine) sugar

115g/4oz/1 cup plain
  (all-purpose) flour

5ml/1 tsp ground cinnamon

1.5ml/¼ tsp ground cloves

1.5ml/¼ tsp ground nutmeg

1.5ml/¼ tsp ground cardamom

275g/10oz/2 cups unblanched
  almonds, coarsely ground

25g/1oz/¼ cup candied lemon
  peel, finely chopped

25g/1oz/¼ cup candied orange
  peel, finely chopped

40g/1½oz plain (semisweet)
  chocolate, grated

2.5ml/½ tsp grated lemon rind

2.5ml/½ tsp grated orange rind

10ml/2 tsp rosewater

1 egg white

10ml/2 tsp cocoa powder, mixed
  with 15ml/1 tbsp boiling water

115g/4oz/generous 1 cup
  icing (confectioners') sugar

30ml/2 tbsp sugar crystals

1 Preheat the oven to 160°C/325°F/
Gas 3. Base-line a 30 x 23cm/12 x 9in
Swiss (jelly) roll tin (pan) with rice paper.

2 Whisk the eggs and caster sugar in
a large bowl until thick and pale. Sift
the flour, cinnamon, ground cloves,
nutmeg and cardamom. Stir in all the
remaining dry ingredients.

3 Spread in the prepared tin and
brush with the rosewater. Bake for
30–35 minutes until firm.

4 Make the icing. Stir the egg white
into the cooled cocoa mixture, sift
in the icing sugar and mix. Spread over
the cake while still warm. Sprinkle
with sugar crystals. Return to the oven
for 5 minutes. Cut into squares when cold.

COOK'S TIP

*Do not worry when the top of the
cake cracks when you cut it; it is
meant to be like that!*

DESSERTS

Pear Tart Tatin
with Cardamom

Cardamom is a spice that is equally at home in sweet and savoury dishes. It is delicious with pears.

SERVES 2–4

50g/2oz/¼ cup butter, softened
60ml/4 tbsp caster (superfine) sugar
seeds from 10 cardamoms
225g/8oz puff pastry, thawed
 if frozen
3 ripe pears
cream, to serve

1 Preheat the oven to 220°C/425°F/ Gas 7. Spread the butter over the base of an 18cm/7in heavy cake tin (pan) or an ovenproof omelette pan. Spread the sugar evenly over the base of the tin or pan. Sprinkle the cardamom seeds over the sugar. On a floured surface, roll out the pastry to a circle slightly larger than the tin or pan. Prick the pastry lightly, support it on a baking sheet and chill.

2 Peel the pears, cut out the cores and slice them lengthways into halves. Arrange the pears, rounded side down, on the butter and sugar. Set the cake tin or omelette pan over a medium heat until the sugar melts and begins to bubble with the butter and juice from the pears. If any areas are browning more than others, move the pan, but do not stir.

3 As soon as the sugar has caramelized, remove the tin or pan carefully from the heat. Place the pastry on top, tucking the edges down the side of the pan. Transfer to the oven and bake for 25 minutes until the pastry is well risen and golden.

4 Leave the tart in the tin or pan for 2–3 minutes until the juices have stopped bubbling. Invert the tin over a plate and shake to release the tart. It may be necessary to slide a spatula underneath the pears to loosen them. Serve the tart warm with cream.

COOK'S TIP

Choose fairly large round pears for this tart, rather than the more elongated varieties.

Pumpkin Pie

This pie is served at Thanksgiving, or at Hallowe'en to use the pulp from the pumpkin lanterns.

SERVES 8

200g/7oz/1¾ cups plain
  (all-purpose) flour
90g/3½ oz/scant ½ cup unsalted
  (sweet) butter
1 egg yolk
900g/2lb piece of pumpkin
2 large (US extra large) eggs
75g/3oz/6 tbsp light brown sugar
60ml/4 tbsp golden (light
  corn) syrup
250ml/8fl oz/1 cup double
  (heavy) cream
15ml/1 tbsp mixed (pumpkin
  pie) spice
salt
icing (confectioners') sugar,
  to decorate

1 Sift the flour and 2.5ml/½ tsp salt into a mixing bowl. Rub in the butter until the mixture resembles breadcrumbs, then mix in the yolk and enough iced water (about 15ml/1 tbsp) to make a dough. Roll the dough into a ball, wrap in clear film (plastic wrap) and chill for at least 30 minutes.

2 Make the filling. Peel the pumpkin and remove the seeds. Cut the flesh into cubes. Place in a heavy pan and add water to cover. Bring to the boil and cook until tender. Mash until completely smooth, then leave in a sieve set over a bowl to drain thoroughly.

3 Roll out the pastry on a lightly floured surface and line a 23–25cm/9–10in loose-based flan tin (tart pan). Prick the base and line with baking parchment and baking beans. Chill for 15 minutes. Preheat the oven to 200°C/400°F/Gas 6. Bake for 10 minutes, remove the parchment and beans, return the tin to the oven and bake for 5 minutes more.

4 Lower the oven temperature to 190°C/375°F/Gas 5. Tip the pumpkin pulp into a bowl and beat in the eggs, sugar, syrup, cream, mixed spice and 2.5ml/½ tsp salt. Pour the mixture into the pastry case (pie shell). Bake for 40 minutes or until the filling has set. Dust with icing sugar and serve at room temperature.

Clementines with Star Anise and Cinnamon

This fresh dessert, delicately flavoured with mulling spices, makes the perfect ending for a festive meal.

SERVES 6

350ml/12fl oz/1½ cups sweet dessert wine
90ml/6 tbsp caster (superfine) sugar
6 star anise
1 cinnamon stick
1 vanilla pod (bean)
1 strip of thinly pared lime rind
30ml/2 tbsp Cointreau
12 clementines

1 Put the wine, sugar, star anise and cinnamon in a pan. Split the vanilla pod and add it to the pan with the lime rind. Bring to the boil, lower the heat and simmer gently for 10 minutes. Allow to cool, then stir in the Cointreau.

2 Peel the clementines, removing all the pith and white membranes. Cut some clementines in half and arrange them all in a glass dish. Pour over the spiced wine and chill overnight.

VARIATION

Tangerines or oranges can be used instead of clementines.

Pistachio Halva Ice Cream

Halva is made from sesame seeds and is available in several flavours. This ice cream, studded with chunks of pistachio-flavoured halva, is as unusual as it is irresistible.

SERVES 6

3 egg yolks
115g/4oz/½ cup caster (superfine) sugar
300ml/½ pint/1¼ cups single (light) cream
300ml/½ pint/1¼ cups double (heavy) cream
115g/4oz pistachio halva
chopped pistachio nuts, to decorate

1 Turn the freezer to its lowest setting. Whisk the egg yolks with the caster sugar in a bowl until thick and pale. Pour the single cream into a small pan and bring to the boil. Stir the hot cream into the egg yolk mixture.

2 Transfer the mixture to a double boiler or a heatproof bowl placed over a pan of boiling water. Cook, stirring constantly, until the custard is thick enough to coat the back of a spoon. Strain into a bowl and leave to cool.

COOK'S TIP

Use an ice-cream maker, if you have one, to freeze the ice cream.

3 Whisk the double cream lightly, then whisk in the cooled custard. Crumble the halva into the mixture and stir in gently.

4 Pour the mixture into a freezer-proof container. Cover and freeze for 3 hours or until half set. Stir well, breaking up any ice crystals, then return to the freezer until frozen solid.

5 Remove the ice cream from the freezer about 15 minutes before serving so that it softens enough for scooping, and to allow the full flavour to develop. Decorate with chopped pistachio nuts.

Ginger and Lemon Puddings with Vanilla Custard

The flavours complement each other perfectly in these light little puddings.

SERVES 8

3 lemons
75g/3oz drained stem (crystallized) ginger plus 30ml/ 2 tbsp syrup from the jar
60ml/4 tbsp golden (light corn) syrup
175g/6oz/1½ cups self-raising (self-rising) flour
10ml/2 tsp ground ginger
115g/4oz/½ cup butter, softened
115g/4oz/½ cup caster (superfine) sugar
2 eggs, beaten
200ml/7 fl oz/scant 1 cup milk
150ml/¼ pint/⅔ cup double (heavy) cream
1 vanilla pod (bean), split
3 egg yolks
5ml/1 tsp cornflour (cornstarch)
30ml/2 tbsp caster (superfine) sugar

1 Preheat the oven to 160°C/325°F/ Gas 3. Grease 8 individual heatproof bowls. Set 1 lemon aside for the sauce. Grate the rind from the remaining lemons and reserve in a bowl. Remove all the pith from one of the grated lemons and slice the flesh into 8 thin rounds. Squeeze the juice from the second grated lemon. Finely chop the stem ginger.

2 In a bowl, mix 15ml/1 tbsp of the ginger syrup with 30ml/2 tbsp of the golden syrup and 5ml/1 tsp of the lemon juice. Divide among the greased bowls. Place a slice of lemon in the bottom of each of the bowls.

3 Sift the flour and ground ginger into a bowl. In a separate bowl, beat the butter and sugar together until pale and fluffy. Gradually beat in the eggs, then fold in the flour mixture and add enough milk to give a soft dropping (pourable) consistency. Stir in the reserved grated lemon rind. Spoon into the prepared bowls.

4 Cover each bowl with foil and stand in a roasting pan. Add boiling water to come halfway up the bowls. Overwrap with foil, sealing well. Bake for 30–45 minutes, until cooked through.

5 Meanwhile make a lemon and ginger sauce. Grate the rind and squeeze the juice from the remaining lemon. Place in a pan with the remaining ginger syrup and golden syrup. Bring to the boil, lower the heat and simmer for 2 minutes. Keep warm.

6 Make the vanilla custard. Mix the remaining milk and the cream in a pan. Add the vanilla pod. Heat to just below boiling. Remove from the heat and leave for 10 minutes. Whisk together the yolks, cornflour and sugar until light, then strain in the hot milk and cream. Whisk until blended, return to the clean pan and heat, stirring, until thick. Turn out the puddings, spoon over the sauce and serve with the custard.

Churros with Cinnamon Syrup

Deep-fried choux puffs tossed in sugar flavoured with star anise are a popular Mexican dessert. They are traditionally served with a cinnamon syrup.

SERVES 4–6

50g/2oz/¼ cup unsalted
 (sweet) butter
65g/2½oz/⅔ cup plain
 (all-purpose) flour, sifted
2 eggs, beaten
oil, for deep-frying
shreds of pared orange rind,
 to decorate
STAR ANISE SUGAR
5 star anise
90ml/6 tbsp caster (superfine) sugar
CINNAMON SYRUP
115g/4oz/½ cup caster
 (superfine) sugar
2 star anise
1 cinnamon stick
30ml/2 tbsp orange juice

1 Make the star anise sugar. Grind the star anise and sugar in a mortar with a pestle until fine. Sift into a bowl.

2 To make the cinnamon syrup, mix the sugar and 150ml/¼ pint/⅔ cup water in a pan. Add the star anise and cinnamon stick. Heat, stirring occasionally until the sugar has dissolved, then boil without stirring for 2 minutes. Stir in the orange juice and set aside.

3 Melt the butter in a pan. Add 150ml/¼ pint/⅔ cup water and bring to the boil. Add the flour, all at once, and beat thoroughly until the mixture leaves the sides of the pan. Let cool slightly, then vigorously beat in the eggs, a little at a time. Spoon the churro mixture into a large piping (pastry) bag with a large star nozzle.

4 Heat the oil to 180°C/350°F or until a cube of bread browns in 1 minute. Fry a few churros at a time: pipe the paste into the oil, cutting off 2.5cm/1in lengths with a knife. Each batch will take 3–4 minutes. The churros are ready when they float to the surface of the oil and are golden. Drain the churros on kitchen paper and keep hot while you are cooking successive batches.

5 Toss the churros in the star anise sugar. Decorate with the shreds of orange rind. Pour the cinnamon syrup into a small bowl and serve with the hot churros.

Kulfi with Cardamom

Kulfi is a delicately spiced Indian ice cream, which is traditionally made in individual containers. Yogurt pots or dariole moulds are ideal, but it can be made like other ice cream in a large container if you prefer.

SERVES 6

2 litres/3½ pints/8 cups full-cream (whole) milk
12 cardamoms
175g/6oz/¾ cup caster (superfine) sugar
25g/1oz/¼ cup blanched almonds, chopped
toasted flaked (sliced) almonds and cardamoms, to decorate

1 Place the milk and cardamoms in a large, heavy pan. Bring to the boil, then simmer vigorously until reduced by one-third. Strain the milk into a bowl, discarding the cardamoms, then stir in the sugar and almonds until the sugar is dissolved. Cool.

COOK'S TIP

Use a large pan for reducing the milk, as there needs to be plenty of room for it to bubble up.

2 Pour the mixture into a freezer-proof container, cover and freeze until almost firm, stirring every 30 minutes. When almost solid, pack the ice cream into six clean yogurt pots. Return to the freezer until required, removing the pots about 10 minutes before serving and turning the individual ices out. Decorate with toasted almonds and cardamoms before serving.

Pears in Mulled Wine

The red wine gives the pears a deep ruby colour, and the spices contribute a lovely warm flavour.

SERVES 4

1 bottle full-bodied red wine
1 cinnamon stick
4 cloves
2.5ml/½ tsp grated nutmeg
2.5ml/½ tsp ground ginger
8 peppercorns
175g/6oz/¾ cup caster (superfine) sugar
thinly pared rind of ½ orange
thinly pared rind of ½ lemon
8 firm ripe pears

1 Pour the wine into a heavy pan into which the pears will fit snugly when standing upright. Stir the cinnamon stick, cloves, nutmeg, ground ginger, peppercorns, caster sugar and citrus rinds into the wine.

COOK'S TIP

Serve the pears with a mascarpone cream, made by combining equal quantities of mascarpone cheese and double (heavy) cream, and adding a little vanilla essence (extract).

2 Peel the pears, leaving the stalks intact, and stand them in the pan. The wine should only just cover the pears. Bring the liquid to the boil, lower the heat, cover and simmer very gently for 30 minutes or until the pears are tender. Using a slotted spoon, transfer the pears to a bowl.

3 Boil the poaching liquid until it has reduced by half and is syrupy. Strain the syrup over and around the pears and serve hot or cold.

PRESERVES AND CHUTNEYS

Moroccan Spiced Preserved Lemons

Salt is all that you need to preserve lemons, but adding spices gives them an aromatic flavour.

MAKES ABOUT 900G/2LB

6 unwaxed lemons, washed
90ml/6 tbsp sea salt
30ml/2 tbsp black peppercorns
4 bay leaves
6 cardamoms
1 cinnamon stick
sunflower oil

1 Cut the lemons lengthwise into quarters. Layer the lemon quarters and salt in a sieve, place over a bowl and leave to drain for 2 days.

COOK'S TIP

The chopped preserved peel from preserved lemons is used in couscous, tagines and other Middle Eastern chicken and fish dishes.

2 Pack the lemon quarters tightly into one or two clean preserving jars with the peppercorns, bay leaves, cardamoms and cinnamon stick.

3 Pour in sunflower oil to cover the lemons, seal the jar and leave for 3–4 weeks before using.

Roasted Red Pepper and Chilli Jelly

The hint of chilli in this glowing red jelly makes it ideal for spicing up hot or cold roast meat. The jelly is also good stirred into sauces.

MAKES ABOUT 900G/2LB

8 red (bell) peppers, quartered
and seeded
4 fresh red chillies, halved
and seeded
1 onion, roughly chopped
2 garlic cloves, roughly chopped
250ml/8fl oz/1 cup water
250ml/8fl oz/1 cup white
wine vinegar
7.5ml/1½ tsp salt
450g/1lb/2 cups preserving sugar
13g/½oz sachet powdered pectin
(about 25ml/5 tsp)

1 Place the peppers, skin-side up, on a rack in a grill (broiling) pan. Grill (broil) until the skins blister and blacken. Place in a plastic bag until cool enough to handle, then remove the skins.

2 Purée the red peppers with the chillies, onion, garlic and water in a blender or food processor. Press the purée through a nylon sieve set over a bowl, pressing hard with a wooden spoon to extract as much juice as possible. There should be about 750ml/1¼ pints/3 cups.

3 Scrape the purée into a large stainless steel pan. Add the vinegar and salt. In a bowl, mix the sugar and pectin, then stir into the liquid. Heat gently until both the sugar and pectin have dissolved, then bring to a full rolling boil. Boil, stirring frequently, for exactly 4 minutes.

4 Remove the jelly from the heat and pour into warm sterilized jars. Leave to cool and set, then cover.

COOK'S TIP

It is not essential to use preserving sugar, but it produces less scum.

Clementine and Coriander Marmalade

Coriander has a warm spicy flavour, which goes particularly well with clementines and lemons.

MAKES ABOUT 2.75KG/6LB
1.3–1.6kg/3–3¹/₂lb clementines
6 unwaxed lemons
30ml/2 tbsp coriander seeds, roasted and coarsely crushed
1.3–1.6kg/3–3¹/₂lb/6 cups preserving sugar

1 Wash the clementines and lemons, then cut them in half. Squeeze all the fruit and pour the juice into a large pan.

2 Scrape all the pith from the citrus shells and tie it, with the pips (seeds) and half the coriander, in a piece of muslin (cheesecloth). Add to the juice.

3 Slice the clementine and lemon peel into shreds and add them to the pan with 3 litres/5¹/₄ pints/12 cups water.

4 Bring the water to the boil, lower the heat and simmer for 1¹/₂ hours, or until the clementine and lemon peel is very soft. Remove the muslin bag. Holding it over the pan, squeeze it between 2 saucers.

5 Add the sugar and the remaining coriander seeds to the pan and stir over a low heat until dissolved. Boil rapidly until setting point is reached. Skim the surface of the marmalade, then leave it to stand for 30 minutes, stirring occasionally to distribute the peel evenly. Pour into warm sterilized jars and cover with waxed paper discs. Seal the jars when cool and store them in a cool dry place.

> **COOK'S TIP**
>
> *To test for a set, spoon a little marmalade on to a cold saucer. If a wrinkled skin forms within a few minutes it is ready for skimming.*

Spiced Kumquats

Cloves and other spices are combined with kumquats to make a perfect accompaniment for baked ham.

MAKES ABOUT 900G/2LB
500g/1¹/₄lb kumquats
350ml/12fl oz/1¹/₂ cups white wine vinegar
500g/1¹/₄lb/2¹/₂ cups granulated sugar
1 cinnamon stick
15 cloves
6 allspice berries

1 Cut the kumquats into quarters and remove the pips (seeds). Place the kumquats in a large heavy pan and pour in just enough water to cover. Bring to the boil, then lower the heat and simmer gently until all the fruit is tender.

> **COOK'S TIP**
>
> *If you like, tie the spices in a muslin (cheesecloth) bag and remove them before bottling.*

2 With a slotted spoon, remove the kumquats and set them aside. Add the vinegar, sugar, cinnamon stick, cloves and allspice berries to the cooking liquid. Bring to the boil, stirring occasionally. Return the kumquats to the pan, lower the heat and simmer for 30 minutes.

3 With a slotted spoon, remove the kumquats from the syrup and place in warm sterilized jars. Boil the syrup until thick and syrupy. Pour over the kumquats, cover and leave for at least 2 weeks before using.

Fresh Tomato, Onion and Coriander Chutney

Indian chutneys of this type are not meant to be kept, but are used in much the same way as salsas, and eaten when freshly made. Fresh chilli is used with cayenne pepper to make the relish quite hot.

COOK'S TIP

If red onions aren't available, use a mild white onion or two or three shallots instead. Serve the chutney with poppadums as an appetizer as guests sit down to an Indian meal.

SERVES 4–6

2 tomatoes
1 red onion
1 fresh green chilli, seeded and finely chopped
60ml/4 tbsp chopped fresh coriander (cilantro)
juice of 1 lime
2.5ml/$\frac{1}{2}$ tsp salt
2.5ml/$\frac{1}{2}$ tsp ground paprika
2.5ml/$\frac{1}{2}$ tsp cayenne pepper
2.5ml/$\frac{1}{2}$ tsp cumin seeds, roasted and ground

1 Dice the tomatoes and onion finely. Place them in a bowl.

2 Add the chilli, coriander, lime juice, salt, paprika, cayenne and cumin seeds. Mix well and serve as soon as possible.

Bread and Butter Pickles

This is a traditional American pickle with a distinctive blend of whole spices. The celery seeds combine particularly well with the cucumber, and the mustard seeds add a little fire and also look attractive in the jar.

MAKES ABOUT 1.8–2KG/4–4$\frac{1}{2}$LB

900g/2lb cucumbers, cut into 5mm/$\frac{1}{4}$in slices
2 onions, thinly sliced
50g/2oz/$\frac{1}{4}$ cup salt
350ml/12fl oz/1$\frac{1}{2}$ cups cider vinegar
350g/12oz/1$\frac{1}{2}$ cups granulated sugar
30ml/2 tbsp white mustard seeds
10ml/2 tsp celery seeds
2.5ml/$\frac{1}{2}$ tsp ground turmeric
2.5ml/$\frac{1}{2}$ tsp black peppercorns

1 Put the cucumbers and onions in a large bowl. Add the salt and mix well. Fit a plate inside the bowl, pressing down on the cucumber mixture. Add a weight to compress the vegetables even more, and leave for 3 hours. Drain the cucumber and onions, rinse under cold running water and drain again.

COOK'S TIP

When making pickles and chutneys, always use a stainless steel or well-coated enamel pan. Avoid aluminium or copper pans as these metals react with the acid in vegetables and fruit.

2 Put the vinegar, sugar, mustard seeds, celery seeds, ground turmeric and peppercorns in a large pan. Bring to the boil, stirring to dissolve the sugar. Add the drained cucumber and onions. As soon as the mixture comes to the boil again, remove the pan from the heat.

3 Spoon the pickle into warm sterilized preserving jars, making sure the vegetables are covered with the liquid. Cover with airtight, vinegar-proof lids and store for at least 1 month before using.

Christmas Chutney

This savoury mixture of spices and dried fruit takes its inspiration from mincemeat, and makes a delicious addition to a Christmas buffet.

MAKES 900G–1.6KG / 2–3½LB

450g/1lb cooking apples, peeled, cored and chopped
500g/1¼lb/3 cups luxury mixed dried fruit
grated rind of 1 orange
30ml/2 tbsp mixed spice
150ml/¼ pint/⅔ cup cider vinegar
350g/12oz/2 cups light brown sugar

1 Place the apples, dried fruit and orange rind in a large pan. Stir in the mixed spice, vinegar and sugar. Heat gently, stirring constantly until all the sugar has dissolved.

> **COOK'S TIP**
>
> *Watch the chutney carefully towards the end of the cooking time, as it has a tendency to catch on the base of the pan. Stir frequently at this stage.*

2 Bring to the boil, then lower the heat and simmer, for 40–45 minutes, stirring occasionally, until the mixture is thick. Ladle into warm sterilized jars, cover and seal. Keep for 1 month before using.

Green Tomato Chutney

This is a classic chutney to make at the end of summer when the last tomatoes on the plants refuse to ripen. Preparing your own pickling spice makes it easy to add exactly the right amount of spiciness to balance the sweet and sour flavours.

MAKES ABOUT 2.5KG / 5½LB

1.75kg/4–4½ lb green tomatoes, coarsely chopped
450g/1lb cooking apples, peeled, cored and chopped
450g/1lb onions, chopped
2 large garlic cloves, crushed
15ml/1 tbsp salt
45ml/3 tbsp pickling spice
600ml/1 pint/2½ cups cider vinegar
450g/1lb/2 cups granulated sugar

1 Place the tomatoes, apples, onions and garlic in a pan. Add the salt. Tie the pickling spice in a piece of muslin (cheesecloth) and add to the pan.

2 Pour in half the vinegar and bring to the boil. Lower the heat and simmer for 1 hour, or until the chutney is thick, stirring frequently.

3 Dissolve the sugar in the remaining vinegar and add to the chutney. Simmer for 1½ hours until the chutney is thick, stirring. Remove the muslin bag from the chutney. Spoon the hot chutney into warm sterilized jars. Cover with airtight, vinegar-proof lids and store for at least 1 month before using.

> **COOK'S TIP**
>
> *Use a jam funnel to transfer the chutney into the jars. Wipe the jars and label them when cold.*

Index

A 🍂

aioli, piri-piri prawns with 32
allspice
  Caribbean fish steaks 28
  glazed sweet potatoes with ginger and
    allspice 66
almonds
  chocolate lebkuchen 105
apples
  apple and cinnamon muffins 102
  Christmas chutney 124
apricots
  lamb tagine 54
  roast lamb with apricot, cinnamon and
    cumin stuffing 52
  turkey sosaties with a curried apricot
    sauce 40
avocados
  tsire koftas with avocado and melon
    salsa 58

B 🍂

beef
  beef teriyaki 50
  black bean chilli con carne 51
  pastitsio 78
blachan 7
black bean chilli con carne 51
black bean sauce, stir-fried five spice squid
  with 31
bread
  chilli cornbread 90
  focaccia with green peppercorns and
    rock salt 88
  spiced naan bread 89
bread and butter pickles 122
brioches, orange and coriander 95
bruising spices 7
bulgur wheat
  bulgur wheat and lentil pilaff 85
  roast lamb with apricot, cinnamon and
    cumin stuffing 52
buns
  Chelsea buns 92
  Cornish saffron buns 92
butternut squash soup with curried
  horseradish cream 16

C 🍂

Cajun spice mix 10
  Cajun blackened fish with papaya
    salsa 28
  jambalaya 81
cakes
  chocolate lebkuchen 105
  ginger cake 101
  honey spice cake 99

lemon poppy seed cake 100
spiced Caribbean Christmas cake 98
vanilla streusel bars 104
capers
  marinated feta cheese with capers 20
  Spanish salad with capers and olives 70
caraway seeds, paprika pork with fennel
  and 59
cardamoms
  kulfi with cardamom 114
  pear tart tatin with cardamom 108
  pilau rice with whole spices 82
Caribbean Christmas cake, spiced 98
Caribbean fish steaks 28
cayenne pepper
  Caribbean fish steaks 28
cheese
  chilli cheese muffins 90
  hot pepperoni pizza 79
  marinated feta cheese with capers 20
  pastitsio 78
Chelsea buns 92
chermoula, Marrakesh monkfish with 34
chicken
  chicken with forty cloves of garlic 42
  fragrant chicken curry with Thai
    spices 39
  jambalaya 81
  Moroccan harissa-spiced roast
    chicken 38
  spiced poussins 42
  spicy Indonesian chicken satay 40
  Thai fried rice 82
chickpea and coriander cakes with
  tahini 19
chillies 7
  black bean chilli con carne 51
  Caribbean fish steaks 28
  chilli cheese muffins 90
  chilli cornbread 90
  chilli, tomato and olive pasta 76
  dhal with tadka 65
  hot and sour prawn soup 14
  hot pepperoni pizza 79
  jerk pork 60
  Mexican tortilla parcels 68
  piri-piri prawns with aioli 32
  Provençal fish soup with rouille 15
  roasted red pepper and chilli jelly 118
  spicy potato wedges with chilli dip 22
chocolate lebkuchen 105
chopping spices 7
Christmas cake, spiced Caribbean 98
Christmas chutney 124
churros with cinnamon syrup 113
chutney
  Christmas chutney 124
  fresh tomato, onion and coriander
    chutney 122
  green tomato chutney 124
cilantro *see* coriander leaves
cinnamon
  apple and cinnamon muffins 102
  bulgur wheat and lentil pilaff 85
  Chelsea buns 92
  churros with cinnamon syrup 113
  clementines with star anise and
    cinnamon 110
  green peppercorn and cinnamon
    crusted lamb 53
  pastitsio 78

pears in mulled wine 114
roast lamb with apricot, cinnamon and
  cumin stuffing 52
spiced kumquats 120
stollen 94
clams
  mussels and clams with lemon grass and
    coconut cream 26
clementines
  clementine and coriander
    marmalade 120
  clementines with star anise and
    cinnamon 110
cod
  Caribbean fish steaks 28
  cod and prawn green coconut curry 32
coriander
  baby onions and mushrooms à la
    Grecque 23
  bulgur wheat and lentil pilaff 85
  chickpea and coriander cakes with
    tahini 19
  clementine and coriander
    marmalade 120
  orange and coriander brioches 95
  roasted root vegetables with whole spice
    seeds 66
  spiced poussins 42
coriander leaves
  fresh tomato, onion and coriander
    chutney 122
  Marrakesh monkfish with chermoula 34
cornbread, chilli 90
Cornish saffron buns 92
couscous
  couscous salad 84
  vegetable couscous with saffron and
    harissa 69
crab
  crab cakes with ginger and wasabi 30
  crab spring rolls and dipping sauce 18
crushing spices 7
cumin
  couscous salad 84
  lamb tagine 54
  orange and red onion salad with
    cumin 70
  roast lamb with apricot, cinnamon and
    cumin stuffing 52
  roasted root vegetables with whole spice
    seeds 66
  spiced poussins 42
curries
  butternut squash soup with curried
    horseradish cream 16
  cod and prawn green coconut curry 32
  fragrant chicken curry with Thai
    spices 39
  seven-seas curry powder 11
  turkey sosaties with a curried apricot
    sauce 40
  vegetable korma 64

D 🍂

dhal with tadka 65
dolmades, spiced 20
dried fruit
  Chelsea buns 92
  Christmas chutney 124
  spiced Caribbean Christmas cake 98

Acknowledgements

Lesley Mackley would like to thank her
family and friends for their willingness to
try out new recipes, with special thanks to
Edward Shaw of Bart Spices for his
invaluable help and advice.

The Publishers would like to thank the
following companies who supplied spices
and equipment for photography:
Cool Chili Company, PO Box 5702,
London W10 6WE, Tel. 020 7229 9360;
Bart Spices Limited, York Road,
Bedminster, Bristol, BS3 4AD,
0117 977 3474; Pepper Alley Herbs,
Fiddes Payne Limited, The Spice
Warehouse, Banbury, Oxfordshire, OX16
8JB, Tel. 01295 253 888; Magimix UK
Limited, 115A High Street Godalming,
Surrey, GU7 1AQ, Tel. 01483 427411.